Buckwheat F
103 Flour Recipes

Foodie's Feast House Saku

Copyright © 2023 Foodie's Feast House Saku
All rights reserved.

Contents

INTRODUCTION 7
1. Buckwheat Pancakes 9
2. Buckwheat Waffles 10
3. Buckwheat Banana Bread 11
4. Buckwheat Chocolate Chip Cookies 12
5. Buckwheat Blueberry Muffins 12
6. Buckwheat Cinnamon Rolls 14
7. Buckwheat Crepes 15
8. Buckwheat Pizza Crust 15
9. Buckwheat Tortillas 16
10. Buckwheat Scones 17
11. Buckwheat Gingerbread 18
12. Buckwheat Biscuits 19
13. Buckwheat Crackers 20
14. Buckwheat Apple Cake 21
15. Buckwheat Brownies 22
16. Buckwheat Bagels 23
17. Buckwheat Bread 24
18. Buckwheat Zucchini Bread 25
19. Buckwheat Pumpkin Muffins 26
20. Buckwheat Cornbread 27
21. Buckwheat Chocolate Cake 28
22. Buckwheat Shortbread Cookies 29
23. Buckwheat Granola Bars 30
24. Buckwheat Cereal 31
25. Buckwheat Energy Balls 32
26. Buckwheat Pie Crust 33
27. Buckwheat Dumplings 34

28. Buckwheat Noodles 35

29. Buckwheat Stir-Fry 36

30. Buckwheat Salad 37

31. Buckwheat Stuffed Peppers 38

32. Buckwheat Veggie Burgers 39

33. Buckwheat Falafel 40

34. Buckwheat Pilaf 41

35. Buckwheat Risotto 42

36. Buckwheat Tabbouleh 42

37. Buckwheat Stuffed Mushrooms 43

38. Buckwheat Stuffed Tomatoes 45

39. Buckwheat Veggie Wraps 46

40. Buckwheat Sushi Rolls 47

41. Buckwheat Veggie Stir-Fry 48

42. Buckwheat Fried Rice 49

43. Buckwheat Spring Rolls 49

44. Buckwheat Pancake Tacos 50

45. Buckwheat Breakfast Burritos 51

46. Buckwheat Quesadillas 52

47. Buckwheat Enchiladas 53

48. Buckwheat Empanadas 54

49. Buckwheat Pierogies 55

50. Buckwheat Gnocchi 56

51. Buckwheat Polenta 57

52. Buckwheat Crusted Chicken 58

53. Buckwheat Fish Fillets 59

54. Buckwheat Meatballs 60

55. Buckwheat Veggie Loaf 61

56. Buckwheat Lentil Soup 62

57. Buckwheat Tomato Soup 63
58. Buckwheat Minestrone 64
59. Buckwheat Mushroom Soup 65
60. Buckwheat Pumpkin Soup 66
61. Buckwheat Chili 67
62. Buckwheat Curry 68
63. Buckwheat Coconut Curry 68
64. Buckwheat Lentil Curry 70
65. Buckwheat Vegetable Curry 71
66. Buckwheat Tofu Stir-Fry 72
67. Buckwheat Quiche 73
68. Buckwheat Spinach Pie 74
69. Buckwheat Stuffed Bell Peppers 75
70. Buckwheat Ratatouille 76
71. Buckwheat Stuffed Eggplant 77
72. Buckwheat Lasagna 78
73. Buckwheat Ravioli 79
74. Buckwheat Mac and Cheese 80
75. Buckwheat Grits 81
76. Buckwheat Stuffed Cabbage Rolls 82
77. Buckwheat Shepherd's Pie 83
78. Buckwheat Chili Mac 84
79. Buckwheat Sloppy Joes 85
80. Buckwheat Tacos 86
81. Buckwheat Burritos 87
82. Buckwheat Eggplant Parmesan 88
83. Buckwheat Stuffed Squash 89
84. Buckwheat Artichoke Dip 90
85. Buckwheat Spinach Dip 91

86. Buckwheat Hummus 92

87. Buckwheat Guacamole 93

88. Buckwheat Salsa 94

89. Buckwheat Cucumber Salad 94

90. Buckwheat Caprese Salad 95

91. Buckwheat Coleslaw 96

92. Buckwheat Potato Salad 97

93. Buckwheat Quinoa Salad 98

94. Buckwheat Tabouli Salad 99

95. Buckwheat Broccoli Salad 100

96. Buckwheat Beet Salad 101

97. Buckwheat Avocado Salad 102

98. Buckwheat Kale Salad 103

99. Buckwheat Brussels Sprouts Salad 104

100. Buckwheat Pear Salad 105

101. Buckwheat Carrot Cake 106

102. Buckwheat Pecan Pie 106

103. Buckwheat Apple Crisp 107

CONCLUSION 109

INTRODUCTION

Buckwheat flour is a nutritious, healthy, and tasty alternative to traditional wheat flour, offering a unique flavor to baked goods and savory meals alike. It has become a popular addition to diets due to its high protein content, and its versatility in cooking. With Buckwheat Bonanza: 103 Flour Recipes, you can explore the wide range of recipes that can be made with buckwheat flour.

This cookbook offers 103 delicious and nutritious recipes that showcase all the wonderful things that can be made with buckwheat flour, including homemade crepes, sweet pastries, gluten-free pancakes, muffins, bread, and so much more. Not only are these recipes healthy, but they are also incredibly delicious – sure to satisfy everyone's taste buds.

The recipes are organized according to type, making it easy to find something that suits your dietary needs and food preferences. Whether you are looking for a quick breakfast or a special dinner, this book has something for you.

With its focus on the health benefits of buckwheat flour, Buckwheat Bonanza not only showcases the flavor of the grain but also lets you explore the numerous health advantages of using it as your primary flour. Buckwheat is a superior alternative to wheat in terms of its high protein and fiber content, low-fat content, and its abundance of essential vitamins and minerals. Buckwheat is naturally gluten-free, making it perfect for those with dietary restrictions, and it is also known for its low glycemic index, meaning the food is steady and sustained energy throughout the day. This cookbook will show you how to take advantage of this unique and nutritious flour to make delicious meals.

In addition to the impressive range of recipes, the book also contains useful information about how to properly store and handle buckwheat flour, as well as how to make substitutions with other flours. There are even helpful tips for troubleshooting any potential baking blunders.

Whether you are an experienced cook or just beginning to learn about the wonders of buckwheat, Buckwheat Bonanza: 103 Flour Recipes provides an amazing selection of recipes that everyone is sure to enjoy. With its delicious recipes and nutritional information, this book will revolutionize the way you think about cooking with buckwheat flour. So, grab a bag of buckwheat flour and let's start cooking!

1. Buckwheat Pancakes

Buckwheat Pancakes are a delicious treat that can be enjoyed for breakfast, brunch or dessert. They are packed with protein, fiber and vitamins and can be made sweet or savory. Enjoy these pancakes in a variety of ways with your favorite toppings.
Serving: Makes 4-6 pancakes
Preparation Time: 10 minutes
Ready Time: 20 minutes

Ingredients:
-1/2 cup buckwheat flour
-1 teaspoon baking powder
-1/4 teaspoon salt
-1 tablespoon sugar
-2 tablespoons vegetable oil
-1 cup non-dairy milk
-1 teaspoon vanilla
-Pinch of cinnamon

Instructions:
1. In a large bowl, combine the buckwheat flour, baking powder, salt, and sugar. Mix well.
2. In a separate bowl, whisk together the oil, milk, vanilla, and cinnamon.
3. Stir the wet Ingredients into the dry Ingredients, mixing until well combined.
4. Heat a lightly oiled griddle over medium heat.
5. Drop ¼-th cup of batter onto the hot griddle, and cook for 1-2 minutes, until the edges are lightly browned and you can see bubbles forming on top.
6. Flip, and cook for another 1-2 minutes, until both sides are lightly browned.
7. Serve with your favorite topping.

Nutrition information: Serving size 1 pancake. Calories 99, Total Fat 3.7 g, Cholesterol 0 mg, Sodium185 mg, Total Carbs 14.7 g, Dietary Fiber 2.2 g, Sugars 2.5 g, Protein 2.6 g.

2. Buckwheat Waffles

Buckwheat Waffles are a delicious and healthy vegan breakfast that can be served sweet or savory. They are light and fluffy on the inside and slightly crispy on the outside, making them a perfect morning treat!
Serving: Eight
Preparation Time: 10 minutes
Ready Time: 20 minutes

Ingredients:
2 cups buckwheat flour
2 teaspoons baking powder
Pinch of salt
1 cup plant-based milk
2 tablespoons melted vegan butter
2 tablespoons pure maple syrup

Instructions:
1. Preheat your waffle maker according to the manufacturer's instructions.
2. In a large bowl, whisk together the buckwheat flour, baking powder, and salt.
3. In a small bowl, combine the plant-based milk, melted vegan butter, and pure maple syrup.
4. Slowly add the wet ingredients to the dry ingredients, stirring until fully absorbed.
5. Prepare the waffles in the preheated waffle maker according to the manufacturer's instructions.
6. Serve hot with favorite toppings or store in the refrigerator for later use.

Nutrition information:
 per Serving: Calories: 211
Fat: 8 g
Carbohydrates: 27 g
Protein: 6 g
Fiber: 2 g
Sugar: 5 g

3. Buckwheat Banana Bread

This Buckwheat Banana Bread is a delicious, fluffy, and moist vegan-friendly banana bread that the whole family is sure to love.
Serving: This recipe serves 8-10 people.
Preparation Time
15 minutes
Ready time: 45 minutes

Ingredients:
- 3 ripe bananas
- 1 cup buckwheat flour
- 1/2 cup coconut sugar
- 1 teaspoon baking soda
- 1 teaspoon baking powder
- 1/2 teaspoon salt
- 1/4 cup coconut oil, melted
- 1/4 cup unsweetened almond milk
- 1 teaspoon vanilla extract

Instructions:
1. Preheat the oven to 350°F (175°C). Grease an 8x4 inch loaf pan with coconut oil.
2. In a medium bowl, mash the bananas with a fork until smooth.
3. Add in the buckwheat flour, coconut sugar, baking soda, baking powder, and salt.
4. In a small bowl, whisk together the melted coconut oil, almond milk, and vanilla extract.
5. Pour the wet Ingredients into the dry Ingredients and mix until blended.
6. Pour the batter into the prepared loaf pan and bake for 40–45 minutes, or until a toothpick comes out clean.
7. Let cool in the pan for 10 minutes before transferring onto a wire rack to cool completely.

Nutrition information
Per Serving: 217 calories; 12.2 g fat; 27 g carbohydrates; 4.3 g protein

4. Buckwheat Chocolate Chip Cookies

These Buckwheat Chocolate Chip Cookies have an incredible flavor thanks to the buckwheat flour, and they are an ideal treat for those who are gluten free!
Serving: Makes 12 cookies
Preparation time: 15 minutes
Ready time: 25 minutes

Ingredients:
- ¾ cup buckwheat flour
- ¼ tsp baking soda
- ¼ teaspoon sea salt
- ¼ cup coconut oil
- ½ cup coconut sugar
- ½ teaspoon vanilla extract
- 2 tablespoons dark chocolate chips

Instructions:
1. Preheat oven to 350°F. Line a baking sheet with parchment paper.
2. In a medium bowl, whisk together the buckwheat flour, baking soda, and salt.
3. In a separate bowl, mix together the coconut oil with the coconut sugar until light and fluffy, then add in the vanilla extract.
4. Slowly add the dry Ingredients to the wet Ingredients, stirring until everything is combined.
5. Fold in the chocolate chips.
6. Roll into 12 balls and place on the baking sheet.
7. Bake for 10-12 minutes.
8. Let cool.

Nutrition information: Per cookie: 125 calories, 8g fat, 14g carbs, 1g protein, 2g fiber

5. Buckwheat Blueberry Muffins

Start your day with delicious and nutritious Buckwheat Blueberry Muffins! Made using buckwheat flour and juicy blueberries, these muffins are easy to make and are sure to please everyone.
Serving: 12 muffins
Preparation time: 10 minutes
Ready time: 25 minutes

Ingredients:
- 2 cups buckwheat flour
- 1/4 cup light brown sugar
- 1 teaspoon baking powder
- 1/2 teaspoon baking soda
- 1/2 teaspoon salt
- 1/2 cup milk
- 1/4 cup vegetable oil
- 1/4 cup honey
- 2 eggs
- 1 teaspoon vanilla extract
- 1 1/2 cups fresh or frozen blueberries

Instructions:
1. Preheat oven to 375°F. Line a 12-cup muffin tin with paper liners.
2. In a large bowl, whisk together buckwheat flour, sugar, baking powder, baking soda, and salt.
3. In a separate bowl, whisk together milk, oil, honey, eggs, and vanilla extract.
4. Pour wet Ingredients into dry Ingredients and stir until just combined.
5. Gently fold in blueberries.
6. Divide batter evenly among muffin cups, filling each cup about 2/3 full.
7. Bake for 18-20 minutes, or until muffin tops are golden brown and a toothpick inserted into center of a muffin comes out clean.
8. Let cool before serving.

Nutrition information:
Calories: 140, Fat: 4g, Carbohydrates: 22g, Protein: 3g, Sodium: 190mg

6. Buckwheat Cinnamon Rolls

Packed with protein and whole grains, this Buckwheat Cinnamon Roll recipe is sure to become a family favorite! Perfectly sweet and spiced, with a delicious cream cheese glaze, these rolls make a special treat for breakfast or dessert.
Serving: 8 rolls
Preparation time: 10 minutes
Ready time: 45 minutes

Ingredients:
- 1 cup lukewarm water
- 1/4 cup warm vegan butter, melted
- 1 teaspoon active dry yeast
- 1/4 cup maple syrup
- 1/4 cup buckwheat flour
- 1 cup oat flour
- 2 tablespoons ground cinnamon
- 1 teaspoon sea salt
- 1/4 cup raisins
- 2 tablespoons melted vegan butter, for topping

Instructions:

1. Preheat your oven to 350°F.
2. In a large bowl, whisk together the warm water, melted butter, and yeast. Let sit for 5 minutes.
3. Add the maple syrup, buckwheat flour, oat flour, cinnamon, and salt. Stir together until combined.
4. Knead the dough for about 5 minutes, adding more flour if needed. Knead in the raisins.
5. Roll out the dough on a lightly floured surface to about 10 x 10 inches.
6. Brush melted vegan butter over the dough and spread the ground cinnamon and sugar onto the dough.
7. Roll the dough into a log and cut into 8 even pieces. Place in a greased baking pan.
8. Bake for 25 minutes, or until golden brown.
9. For the glaze, mix together cream cheese, maple syrup, and almond milk. Spread on cooled rolls.

Nutrition information: Per serving: 210 calories; 8.7 g fat; 2.2 g protein; 32.5 g carbohydrates; 7.5 g sugar; 2.1 g fiber

7. Buckwheat Crepes

Buckwheat Crepes is a traditional French pancake made from buckwheat flour. It is simple to prepare, gluten-free, and delicious.
Serving: 8-10 crepes
Preparation time: 10 minutes
Ready time: 30 minutes

Ingredients:
- 1 ½ cups buckwheat flour
- 2 large eggs
- 2 cups milk
- 2 tablespoons oil
- Pinch of salt

Instructions:
1. In a bowl, mix buckwheat flour, eggs, milk, oil and salt.
2. Whisk the mixture with an electric mixer until it is a smooth consistency.
3. Heat a non-stick pan over low-medium heat.
4. When the pan is hot, pour about ¼ cup of the mixture onto the pan and spread it out evenly.
5. Cook for about 1-2 minutes per side, flipping the crepes over until both sides are golden.
6. Serve warm.

Nutrition information: Calories 149, Total Fat 7 g, Carbs 14 g, Protein 5 g, Sodium 35 mg, Fiber 1 g, Cholesterol 54 mg

8. Buckwheat Pizza Crust

Buckwheat Pizza Crust is a tasty alternative to the traditional pizza crust. It's made with healthy buckwheat flour and its gluten-free properties make this pizza crust easy to digest.

Serving: 8 slices
Preparation Time: 15 minutes
Ready Time: 45 minutes

Ingredients:
- 2 cups buckwheat flour
- 2 tsp baking powder
- 1/2 tsp sea salt
- 2/3 cup warm water
- 3 tbsp olive oil

Instructions:
1. Preheat oven to 425 F.
2. In a bowl mix together buckwheat flour, baking powder and sea salt.
3. Add warm water and olive oil and mix with a spoon until a dough forms.
4. On a lightly floured surface, knead the dough for 5 minutes.
5. Form into a round and place on a pizza baking sheet.
6. Bake for 25 minutes until the crust is golden.
7. Now add your favorite cheese and toppings to the pizza and bake for an additional 20 minutes until cheese is melted.

Nutrition information: Per slice: Calories: 143, Fat: 5.5gm, Carbohydrates: 17gm, Protein: 3.7gm, Sodium: 193mg.

9. Buckwheat Tortillas

Buckwheat Tortillas are a tasty and healthier twist on traditional wheat-based tortillas made with buckwheat, which is gluten-free and high in fiber. This recipe is simple and easy to follow!
Serving: Makes 8 tortillas
Preparation time: 10 minutes
Ready time: 15 minutes

Ingredients:
2 cups buckwheat flour
1 ½ teaspoon baking powder
½ teaspoon sea salt

2 tablespoons olive oil
¾ cup warm water

Instructions:
1. In a large bowl, mix together buckwheat flour, baking powder, and sea salt.
2. Add olive oil and warm water and then mix until combined.
3. Cover the bowl with a damp towel and let it sit for 10 minutes.
4. After 10 minutes, Preheat oven to 400°F (200°C).
5. Place dough on a floured surface and then form into 8 balls.
6. Using a rolling pin, roll each ball into a round tortilla of desired thickness.
7. Place each tortilla on a baking sheet lined with parchment paper.
8. Cook tortillas for 8-10 minutes, flipping halfway through to ensure an even cook.
9. Enjoy!

Nutrition information: Serving size: 1 tortilla, Calories: 169.2, Fat: 4.2g, Carbs: 29.9, Protein: 4.3g.

10. Buckwheat Scones

These buckwheat scones are fluffy, light and tasty. The nuttiness added by buckwheat flour and the earthy flavor of the honey makes a great combination, and the buckwheat pairs nicely with any type of topping.
Serving: 8 scones
Preparation time: 10 minutes
Ready Time: 25 minutes

Ingredients:
-2 cups buckwheat flour
-1 teaspoon baking powder
-1 teaspoon baking soda
-1/4 teaspoon salt
-1/3 cup cold butter, cut into small cubes
-1/4 cup honey
-1/2 cup Greek yogurt
-1/4 cup whole milk

Instructions:
1. Preheat oven to 400 degrees F.
2. In a large bowl, whisk together buckwheat flour, baking powder, baking soda, and salt.
3. Cut in the butter using a pastry blender or your fingers until you get a coarse crumb consistency.
4. Pour in the honey, yogurt, and milk, and mix with a wooden spoon until the dough just comes together.
5. Turn the dough out onto a lightly floured surface and knead for a few minutes until it becomes smooth.
6. Form the dough into a 1/2-inch thick round and cut out 8 scones, either with a biscuit cutter or by using a knife.
7. Place the scones onto a baking sheet lined with parchment paper and bake for 20-25 minutes, or until lightly golden.
8. Enjoy your buckwheat scones with your favorite topping.

Nutrition information:
Calories: 171, Total Fat: 5g, Saturated Fat: 3g, Cholesterol: 13mg, Sodium: 158mg, Carbohydrates: 23g, Fiber: 2g, Sugar: 8g, Protein: 4g

11. Buckwheat Gingerbread

This Buckwheat Gingerbread recipe is a delicious combination of sweet, spicy, and nutty flavors. The buckwheat flour adds an earthy deliciousness to this gingerbread, while the molasses and spices add a unique flavor. Nutritious and easy to make, this gingerbread is a great treat to enjoy throughout the winter season.
Serving: 10
Preparation Time: 15 minutes
Ready Time: 50 minutes

Ingredients:
- 2 cups buckwheat flour
- 1 cup white sugar
- 1 tsp baking soda
- 2 tsp ground ginger
- 1 tsp ground cinnamon

- ½ tsp ground cloves
- ½ tsp ground cardamom
- ½ cup vegetable oil
- ½ cup molasses
- 2 eggs

Instructions:
1. Preheat oven to 350 degrees F (175 degrees C). Grease a 9x13 inch baking dish.
2. In a large bowl, combine flour, sugar, baking soda, ginger, cinnamon, cloves, and cardamom.
3. In a separate bowl, mix together the oil, molasses, and eggs.
4. Add wet Ingredients to the dry Ingredients and mix until fully combined.
5. Pour mixture into the prepared baking dish.
6. Bake in the preheated oven for 40 to 50 minutes, or until a toothpick inserted into the center comes out clean.

Nutrition information:
Calories: 208 kcal, Carbohydrates: 32 g, Protein: 3 g, Fat: 7 g, Saturated Fat: 2 g, Cholesterol: 31 mg, Sodium: 91 mg, Potassium: 101 mg, Fiber: 1 g, Sugar: 21 g, Vitamin A: 66 IU, Calcium: 18 mg, Iron: 1 mg.

12. Buckwheat Biscuits

Buckwheat Biscuits are a delicious savory treat, made with a combination of buckwheat flour, butter, and diced onions. They can be enjoyed as both a savory snack or an accompaniment to a meal.
Serving: Makes 12 biscuits
Preparation Time: 15 minutes
Ready Time: 40 minutes

Ingredients:
- 2 cups buckwheat flour
- 1/2 cup (1 stick) of butter, diced
- 1/2 white or yellow onion, finely diced
- 1 teaspoon sea salt
- 1 teaspoon baking powder

- Milk or water, as needed
- Optional: chopped fresh herbs such as parsley, chives, or thyme

Instructions:
1. Preheat the oven to 350°F (175°C).
2. In a medium bowl, combine the buckwheat flour, butter, onion, sea salt, and baking powder. Use your hands to mix the Ingredients together until the butter is distributed evenly.
3. Add enough milk or water to bring the dough together into a ball.
4. Turn the dough out onto a lightly-floured surface and knead 2–3 times.
5. Roll the dough out to about ¼-inch thickness (about 6mm). Cut out rounds using a biscuit cutter or a glass. Place the rounds on a lightly-greased baking sheet.
6. Bake for 20–25 minutes, until golden brown and crisp.
7. Serve warm or at room temperature.

Nutrition information: per serving (1 biscuit): Cal- 123, Total Fat- 7.7g, Sodium-273mg, Total Carbs-11.2g, Protein-2.7g.

13. Buckwheat Crackers

Savory buckwheat crackers are the perfect addition to any cheese platter or lunch box. They come together quickly and make a great snack for the whole family!
Serving: Makes 8-10 crackers
Preparation time: 5 minutes
Ready time: 25 minutes

Ingredients:
- 1/4 cup buckwheat flour
- 1/4 teaspoon sea salt
- 2 tablespoons olive oil
- 2 tablespoons warm water

Instructions:
1. Preheat oven to 325°F.
2. In a medium bowl, mix together buckwheat flour and salt.

3. Add in the olive oil and water. Mix together until a dough forms, adding more water if needed.
4. Divide the dough into 8-10 pieces and roll each into a thin circle.
5. Place on a parchment-lined baking sheet and bake for 20-25 minutes until golden brown.
6. Let cool before transferring to a storage container.

Nutrition information: Nutrition per serving (1 cracker): 40 Calories, 3g Fat, 2g Carbs, 1g Protein

14. Buckwheat Apple Cake

This delectable Buckwheat Apple Cake is a fluffy and light cake, made with buckwheat flour and topped with apples and a cinnamon sugar crunch. It's perfect for any time of day– breakfast, snack or dessert!
Serving: Serves 8-10
Preparation time: 10 minutes
Ready time: 40 minutes

Ingredients:
- 1¼ cups buckwheat flour
- 1 teaspoon baking powder
- ¼ teaspoon baking soda
- 1 teaspoon cinnamon
- ¼ teaspoon ground ginger
- ¼ teaspoon ground nutmeg
- ½ teaspoon sea salt
- 2 tablespoons maple syrup
- ¼ cup oil of your choice (avocado, coconut or melted butter)
- 2 tablespoons coconut sugar
- 1 cup unsweetened applesauce
- 2 large apples(any type you prefer!)
- 2 tablespoons melted butter
- 2 teaspoons cinnamon
- 2 tablespoons coconut sugar

Instructions:
1. Preheat oven to 350° F and grease an 8" round cake pan.

2. In a medium bowl, mix together buckwheat flour, baking powder, baking soda, cinnamon, ginger, nutmeg and salt.
3. In a separate bowl mix together maple syrup, oil of your choice and coconut sugar.
4. Add in the applesauce and mix until combined.
5. Mix the wet Ingredients into the dry and mix until a thick batter forms.
6. Pour the batter into the prepared pan and spread out evenly.
7. Peel and slice the apples into thin slices and arrange on top of the cake batter.
8. In a small bowl mix together the melted butter, cinnamon and sugar and spread on top of the apples.
9. Place into the preheated oven and bake for 30-35 minutes or until a toothpick comes out clean when inserted into the center.
10. Let cool before slicing and serving.

Nutrition information: Per Serving - Calories: 172, Total Fat: 7g, Cholesterol: 7mg, Sodium: 105mg, Total Carbohydrate: 25g, Dietary Fiber: 4g, Protein: 3g

15. Buckwheat Brownies

Buckwheat brownies are an easy and delicious twist on the classic bake. These brownies have the familiar chocolatey taste and moist texture that everyone loves, but without the added sugars and fats. They're made from natural buckwheat flour, coconut oil, cocoa, and honey, for a healthier spin on the traditional version.
Serving: 8-10
Preparation time: 10 minutes
Ready time: 25 minutes

Ingredients:
- ½ cup buckwheat flour
- 2 tablespoons cocoa powder
- ¼ teaspoon baking soda
- Pinch of salt
- ¼ cup coconut oil, melted
- 2 tablespoons honey
- ½ cup almond milk

- ½ cup chopped walnuts, optional

Instructions:
1. Preheat oven to 350°F and prepare an 8-inch square baking pan with non-stick spray.
2. In a medium bowl, whisk together the buckwheat flour, cocoa powder, baking soda, and salt.
3. In a separate bowl, add the coconut oil, honey, and almond milk and mix until blended.
4. Pour the wet Ingredients into the dry Ingredients and mix with a rubber spatula until combined.
5. Pour the batter into the baking dish and optionally sprinkle with the chopped walnuts.
6. Bake for 25-30 minutes, or until a toothpick inserted into the center comes out clean.
7. Allow to cool completely before slicing into 8-10 squares.

Nutrition information: each buckwheat brownie contains approximately 130 calories, 8 grams of fat, and 11 grams of carbs.

16. Buckwheat Bagels

Buckwheat bagels are a great way to enjoy a classic bagel flavor with a healthy twist. Our recipe swaps traditional wheat flour for buckwheat flour, making a deliciously dense and nutty bagel. Enjoy them with your favorite cream cheese or make them into sandwiches!
Serving: 4
Preparation time: 35 minutes
Ready time: 1 hour 15 minutes

Ingredients:
- 2 teaspoons active dry yeast
- 1 teaspoon sugar
- 1 1/2 cups warm water
- 1/2 cup buckwheat flour
- 2 teaspoons olive oil
- 2 teaspoons salt
- 3 1/2 cups all-purpose flour

- 1 teaspoon baking soda

Instructions:
1. Preheat oven to 375 F (190 C).
2. In a medium bowl, dissolve yeast and sugar in warm water and let stand 10 minutes until bubbly.
3. In a large bowl, combine buckwheat flour, olive oil, salt, all-purpose flour, and baking soda. Add yeast mixture and stir until a dough forms.
4. Knead the dough on a lightly floured surface for 2-3 minutes.
5. Divide the dough into 4 equal pieces.
6. Roll each piece into a thick rope and shape into a bagel.
7. Place bagels on a baking sheet lined with parchment paper and bake for 20 minutes or until golden brown.
8. Enjoy warm or cool completely and store in an airtight container.

Nutrition information: Calories: 219, Fat: 2.2g, Saturated Fat: 0.3g, Carbohydrates: 41.5g, Fiber: 1.7g, Protein: 7g, Sugar: 1.9g, Sodium: 825mg

17. Buckwheat Bread

Buckwheat Bread is a classic loaf made with buckwheat flour and other simple Ingredients. It is a hearty, nutty, and flavorful bread that pairs beautifully with a variety of dishes and adds a unique element to your dinner table.
Serving: 8 slices
Preparation Time: 15 minutes
Ready time: 70 minutes

Ingredients:
- 2 cups buckwheat flour
- 1 teaspoon baking powder
- 1 teaspoon baking soda
- 1 teaspoon salt
- 1/4 cup olive oil
- 1 1/2 cups warm water

Instructions:

1. Preheat the oven to 375°F.
2. In a large bowl, combine the buckwheat flour, baking powder, baking soda, and salt.
3. In a separate bowl, mix the olive oil and warm water until combined.
4. Add the wet Ingredients to the dry Ingredients and mix until combined.
5. Spray a 9x5 inch loaf pan with non-stick spray and pour the batter into the pan.
6. Bake for 60 minutes or until a knife inserted into the center comes out clean.
7. Let the loaf cool for 10 minutes before slicing.

Nutrition information: Per Serving (1 slice) - 116 calories, 6.7 g fat, 13.8 g carbohydrates, 2.5 g protein.

18. Buckwheat Zucchini Bread

Buckwheat Zucchini Bread is a delicious and healthy bread with a combination of buckwheat and zucchini as its main Ingredients. The texture of this bread is dense and moist with a slight nutty flavor coming through.
Serving: 8
Preparation Time: 15 minutes
Ready Time: 1 hour

Ingredients:
- 2 cups buckwheat flour
- 1 teaspoon baking soda
- 1 teaspoon baking powder
- 1/2 teaspoon salt
- 1/4 cup melted coconut oil
- 1/4 cup honey
- 2 eggs
- 1 teaspoon vanilla extract
- 1 cup grated zucchini
- 1/2 cup chopped walnuts (optional)

Instructions:

1. Preheat oven to 375°F and grease a 9-inch loaf pan.
2. In a large bowl, combine the buckwheat flour, baking soda, baking powder, and salt.
3. In a separate bowl, mix together the coconut oil, honey, eggs, and vanilla extract.
4. Slowly pour the wet Ingredients into the dry Ingredients, stirring to combine.
5. Fold in the zucchini and walnuts (if using).
6. Pour the batter into the prepared pan and bake for 45-50 minutes, or until a toothpick inserted into the center of the bread comes out clean.
7. Let cool before slicing and serving.

Nutrition information: (Per Serving):
Calories: 219, Total Fat: 8 g, Cholesterol: 30 mg, Sodium: 50 mg, Total Carbohydrate: 32 g, Dietary Fiber: 4 g, Protein: 5 g

19. Buckwheat Pumpkin Muffins

Enjoy a delicious and healthy snack with this recipe for Buckwheat Pumpkin Muffins. This gluten free treat is the perfect combination of sweet and savory, and is a great way to enjoy the taste of pumpkin all year round.
Serving: Makes 12 muffins
Preparation Time: 10 minutes
Ready time: 25 minutes

Ingredients:
-1 cup buckwheat flour
-½ cup oat flour
-1 teaspoon baking soda
-1 teaspoon baking powder
-½ teaspoon salt
-¼ teaspoon ground cinnamon
-1 ½ cups canned pumpkin
-½ cup almond milk
-¼ cup melted coconut oil
-½ cup coconut sugar
-1 teaspoon vanilla extract

- ¼ cup pumpkin seeds (optional)

Instructions:
1. Preheat the oven to 375F.
2. Grease or line a muffin pan.
3. In a medium bowl, whisk together the buckwheat flour, oat flour, baking soda, baking powder, salt, and cinnamon.
4. In a separate bowl, mix together the pumpkin, almond milk, melted coconut oil, coconut sugar, and vanilla extract.
5. Add the wet Ingredients to the dry Ingredients and mix until combined.
6. Add the pumpkin seeds (if desired).
7. Scoop the batter into the prepared muffin pan, filling each cup ¾ full.
8. Bake for 25 minutes, or until a toothpick inserted in the center comes out clean.
9. Allow to cool before serving.

Nutrition information:
Calories- 189 per muffin
Fat- 7.3g
Carbohydrates- 25.6g
Protein- 3.4g
Fiber- 3.8g

20. Buckwheat Cornbread

Buckwheat Cornbread is a moist and flavorful cornbread that is packed with nutrition from buckwheat flour and cornmeal. It's a great side for soups, chili, or any savory dish.
Serving: 4
Preparation Time: 10 minutes
Ready Time: 25 minutes

Ingredients:
1 cup buckwheat flour
1 cup cornmeal
1 teaspoon baking powder
1 teaspoon salt

1/4 cup butter, melted
1 cup grated cheddar cheese
3/4 cup milk
1 egg, beaten

Instructions:
1. Preheat oven to 375°F and grease an 8-inch square baking dish.
2. In a medium bowl, whisk together buckwheat flour, cornmeal, baking powder, and salt. Set aside.
3. In a separate bowl, mix together butter, cheddar cheese, milk, and egg.
4. Add wet Ingredients to dry Ingredients and stir until well-combined.
5. Pour batter into prepared pan and spread evenly.
6. Bake for 25 minutes or until a toothpick inserted into the center comes out clean.
7. Let cool in pan before cutting.

Nutrition information:
Calories: 245, Total Fat: 13 g, Saturated Fat: 8 g, Total Carbohydrate: 24 g, Dietary Fiber: 2 g, Protein: 7 g

21. Buckwheat Chocolate Cake

Try this delicious and healthy Buckwheat Chocolate Cake for your special occasions. Its flavorsome and gluten-free recipe will be appreciated by all.
Serving: 8 people
Preparation time: 15 minutes
Ready time: 45 minutes

Ingredients:
- 1 cup buckwheat flour
- ½ cup cocoa powder
- 1 teaspoon baking powder
- ½ teaspoon baking soda
- ½ teaspoon salt
- 1 cup coconut sugar
- ½ cup vegetable oil
- 2 large eggs

- 1 cup almond or oat milk
- ½ cup semisweet chocolate chips

Instructions:
1. Preheat oven to 350°F (177°C). Line an 8-inch baking pan with parchment paper.
2. In a medium-sized bowl, combine the buckwheat flour, cocoa powder, baking powder, baking soda, and salt.
3. In a separate bowl, mix together the coconut sugar, vegetable oil, eggs, and almond or oat milk until combined.
4. Slowly add the wet Ingredients to the bowl with the dry Ingredients and stir until combined.
5. Fold in the chocolate chips and pour the batter into the prepared baking pan. Bake in the preheated oven for 35-45 minutes, or until a toothpick inserted in the center comes out clean.
6. Allow the cake to cool before serving.

Nutrition information: Per Serving: 290 calories, 21.7 g fat, 31.2 g carbohydrates, 4.3 g protein, 5.2 g fiber, 106 mg sodium

22. Buckwheat Shortbread Cookies

Enjoy these Buckwheat Shortbread Cookies, made with nutritious buckwheat flour and sweetened with white sugar. They make a wonderful snack alongside a nice cup of tea!
Serving: 25-30 cookies
Preparation Time: 10 minutes
Ready Time: 25 minutes

Ingredients:
- 1 1/4 cups (150 g) buckwheat flour
- 3 tablespoons (25 g) white sugar
- 1/4 teaspoon salt
- 1/2 cup (115 g) butter, room temperature
- 2 tablespoons (30 ml) water
- 2 tablespoons (15 g) finely chopped toasted hazelnuts

Instructions:

1. Preheat oven to 350°F (175°C).
2. In a medium bowl, whisk together the buckwheat flour, sugar, and salt.
3. Cut the butter into cubes and add to the dry Ingredients. Work with your hands until the Ingredients combine and form a soft dough.
4. Add the water and mix until dough becomes homogeneous.
5. Add the toasted hazelnuts and mix.
6. Make small balls with the dough and place onto a parchment paper-lined baking sheet. Flatten slightly with a fork.
7. Bake for 15-20 minutes, until golden brown.
8. Place cookies onto a wire rack and let cool completely before serving.

Nutrition information:
Serving size 1 cookie (30g), Calories 79, Total Fat 4.4g, Saturated fat 2.7g, Sodium 36.4mg, Total Carbohydrate 8.7g, Dietary Fiber 0.6g, Sugars 3g, Protein 0.7g.

23. Buckwheat Granola Bars

Buckwheat Granola Bars are a flavorful and nutritious snack made with oats and nuts. Raw honey, cinnamon, and a hint of sea salt give these bars a subtle sweetness and flavor. They are an ideal snack to have on hand for breakfast, lunch, or your afternoon pick-me-up.
Serving: Makes 18 bars
Preparation time: 10 minutes
Ready time: 30 minutes

Ingredients:
1 cup old-fashioned oats
1 cup buckwheat groats
1/2 cup almonds, chopped
1/2 cup cashews, chopped
1/4 cup raw honey
1/4 teaspoon ground cinnamon
1/4 teaspoon sea salt

Instructions:
1. Preheat the oven to 350°F (175°C).

2. In a large bowl, combine the oats, buckwheat groats, almonds, and cashews.
3. In a separate bowl, stir together the honey, cinnamon, and sea salt.
4. Pour the honey mixture over the oat mixture and stir until combined.
5. Line a 9x9 inch (23x23 cm) baking pan with parchment paper and spread the granola bar mixture out evenly.
6. Bake for 15-20 minutes, or until the edges are golden brown.
7. Let cool completely before cutting into 18 bars.

Nutrition information: Calories per serving—134; Protein—3 g; Fat—4.7 g; Carbohydrates—20.2 g; Fiber—2.4 g; Sugar—6.8 g.

24. Buckwheat Cereal

Buckwheat Cereal is a delicious and nutritious breakfast option made with raw buckwheat groats, rolled oats, and cinnamon. Paired with fresh fruit, it's a great way to start the day.
Serving: Makes 4 servings
Preparation time: 15 minutes
Ready time: 45 minutes

Ingredients:
- 2 cups raw buckwheat groats
- 1 cup rolled oats
- 1 teaspoon ground cinnamon
- 2 cups almond milk
- 2 tablespoons honey
- 1 cup chopped fresh fruit

Instructions:
1. Preheat oven to 350 degrees Fahrenheit.
2. In a medium bowl, combine buckwheat groats, rolled oats, and cinnamon. Mix until all Ingredients are distributed evenly.
3. Pour the mixture into a greased 9-inch baking dish, and spread out evenly.
4. Bake in the oven for 30 minutes, or until golden and toasted.
5. Remove from oven and let cool.

6. Once cooled, pour the mixture into a large bowl and add almond milk and honey. Stir to combine.
7. Divide the cereal into 4 bowls and top with fruit. Serve immediately.

Nutrition information
- Calories – 228 kcal
- Protein – 8 g
- Fat – 4 g
- Carbohydrates – 50 g
- Fiber – 8 g

25. Buckwheat Energy Balls

Buckwheat Energy Balls are a healthy, flavorful snack made from a combination of oats, dates, nut butter, and buckwheat. They are gluten-free, easy to make, and the perfect snack for on-the-go!
Serving: Makes 12 balls
Preparation Time: 10 minutes
Ready Time: 25 minutes

Ingredients:
- 1 cup gluten-free rolled oats
- ½ cup dates, pitted and roughly chopped
- 1 tablespoon coconut oil
- 2 tablespoons nut butter of choice
- 2 tablespoons buckwheat groats
- ¼ teaspoon ground cinnamon
- 1 teaspoon vanilla extract
- ½ cup shredded coconut

Instructions:
1. In a small bowl, combine the oats, dates, coconut oil, nut butter, buckwheat, cinnamon, and vanilla. Stir until all Ingredients are combined.
2. Form the mixture into 12 balls, about 1-inch in diameter and roll in the shredded coconut.
3. Place the balls on an parchment-lined baking sheet and freeze for about 15 minutes.
4. Store in an airtight container in the fridge for up to one week.

Nutrition information: Per ball - Calories: 109, Fat: 6.6 g, Carbohydrates: 11.5 g, Protein: 2.3 g

26. Buckwheat Pie Crust

This recipe for a Buckwheat Pie Crust is a delicious alternative to the traditional pie crust, and is perfect for those who are looking for a gluten-free option.
Serving: Serves 8
Preparation time: 15 minutes
Ready time: 45 minutes

Ingredients:
1 cup buckwheat flour
½ teaspoon sea salt
½ teaspoon cream of tartar
¼ cup cold vegan butter
3-4 tablespoons very cold water

Instructions:
1. Preheat the oven to 350 degrees F.
2. In a medium-sized bowl, mix together the buckwheat flour, sea salt, and cream of tartar.
3. Cut the vegan butter into the flour mixture with a fork or pastry cutter. Continue to mix until the mixture resembles coarse crumbs.
4. Gradually add in the water to the flour mixture one tablespoon at a time. Continue to mix until the dough pulls away from the sides of the bowl.
5. Place the dough onto a lightly floured surface and knead the dough with your hands.
6. Roll out the dough to desired thinness and then place into a 9-inch pie plate.
7. Prick the surface of the dough with a fork to make small holes.
8. Bake for 25-30 minutes or until golden brown. Allow to cool before filling.

Nutrition information (per serving):

Calories: 150
Fat: 8 g
Carbohydrates: 17 g
Protein: 2 g

27. Buckwheat Dumplings

Buckwheat dumplings are a delicious and versatile dish which can be filled with savory meats, vegetables and herbs or sweet fruits. They make a great comfort food and are loved by many.
Serving: 4
Preparation Time: 20 minutes
Ready Time: 40 minutes

Ingredients:
-1 cup buckwheat, ground into a flour
-1 cup all-purpose flour
-2 eggs
-1 teaspoon baking powder
-1/2 teaspoon salt
-1/2 cup warm water

Instructions:
1. In a large bowl, mix together the buckwheat flour, all-purpose flour, eggs, baking powder and salt.
2. Next slowly add the warm water and mix everything until it forms a slightly sticky dough.
3. Knead the dough for a few minutes until smooth.
4. Cover the dough and set it aside for 15 minutes.
5. After 15 minutes, take the dough and divide into 4 equal parts.
6. Take one of the parts and roll it out to a 1/4 inch thick sheet.
7. Cut out circles of dough using a cookie cutter or a cup.
8. Place 1-2 teaspoons of desired filling into the middle of the circles.
9. Fold the dough along the edges and press the edges together to seal.
10. Place the dumplings onto a lightly greased baking sheet.
11. Bake the dumplings at 375°F for 20-25 minutes or until golden brown.

Nutrition information:
Calories: 144 kcal
Carbohydrates: 28g
Protein: 7g
Fat: 1.2g
Sodium: 217mg
Fiber: 3.6g

28. Buckwheat Noodles

Buckwheat Noodles is a healthy and delicious alternative to pasta. It is a popular dish accompanied with a variety of sauces and dressings. Serve this nutritious meal to friends and family for an enjoyable dining experience.
Serving: 4
Preparation Time: 20 minutes
Ready Time: 40 minutes

Ingredients:
- 2 cups buckwheat noodles
- 2 tablespoons sesame oil
- 1 teaspoon soy sauce
- ½ teaspoon sugar
- 2 cloves garlic, minced
- ½ teaspoon ground ginger
- 2 tablespoons oyster sauce
- 2 tablespoons vegetable oil
- ½ cup onion, sliced
- ½ cup yellow bell pepper, chopped
- ½ cup sliced mushrooms

Instructions:
1. Bring a pot of water to a boil. Add buckwheat noodles and simmer for about 10 minutes. Drain and rinse with cold water and set aside.
2. In a bowl, mix together sesame oil, soy sauce, sugar, garlic, ginger, and oyster sauce. Whisk with a fork and set aside.
3. Heat vegetable oil in a wok or skillet on high heat. Toss in the onion, bell pepper, and mushrooms and stir-fry for 3 to 4 minutes.

4. Push vegetables to the side and add the buckwheat noodles. Pour the sauce mixture over the noodles and vegetables, mix to combine, and stir-fry for 1 to 2 minutes.
5. Plate and serve warm.

Nutrition information: Per serving: 411 calories, 27 g fat, 4 g saturated fat, 4 g protein, 38 g carbohydrates, 5 g sugar.

29. Buckwheat Stir-Fry

Buckwheat Stir-Fry is a savory dish made with buckwheat noodles, vegetables, and a flavorful stir-fry sauce. It's a great vegan-friendly option for a quick dinner.
Serving: Serves 4
Preparation time: 10 minutes
Ready time: 25 minutes

Ingredients:
- 8 ounces buckwheat noodles
- 2 tablespoons olive oil
- 1 cup shredded carrot
- 1 cup chopped bell pepper
- 1 cup diced mushrooms
- 2 cloves garlic, minced
- 2 tablespoons soy sauce
- 2 tablespoons rice vinegar
- 1 teaspoon sesame oil
- 2 tablespoons honey
- 2 tablespoons chopped green onion

Instructions:
1. Cook the buckwheat noodles according to package instructions.
2. Heat the olive oil in a large skillet over medium-high heat.
3. Add the carrot, bell pepper, and mushrooms and cook for 3-5 minutes, stirring occasionally.
4. Add the garlic and cook for 1 minute, stirring often.
5. Add the cooked noodles to the skillet and mix everything together.

6. In a small bowl, whisk together the soy sauce, rice vinegar, sesame oil, honey, and green onion.
7. Pour the sauce over the noodles and vegetables and cook for 1-2 minutes, stirring the mixture until everything is evenly coated.
8. Serve hot.

Nutrition information
Calories: 188, Fat: 6.3g, Protein: 4.7g, Carbohydrates: 27.5g, Sodium: 488mg

30. Buckwheat Salad

This Buckwheat Salad is a delicious, light and nutritious salad perfect for any meal. Packed with crunchy vegetables and a light vinaigrette dressing, this salad is sure to please!
Serving: 4
Preparation Time: 10 minutes
Ready Time: 15 minutes

Ingredients:
- 1 cup buckwheat, cooked
- 1/2 cup corn, fresh or canned
- 1/2 cup cherry tomatoes, cut in half
- 1/2 cup red onion, sliced
- 1/3 cup feta cheese, crumbled
- 1/4 cup fresh basil, chopped
- 2 tablespoons olive oil
- 2 tablespoons apple cider vinegar
- 1 tablespoon maple syrup
- 1 tablespoon Dijon mustard
- Salt and pepper, to taste

Instructions:
1. In a bowl, combine buckwheat, corn, tomatoes, red onion, feta cheese and basil.
2. In a separate bowl, whisk together olive oil, apple cider vinegar, maple syrup, Dijon mustard, salt and pepper.
3. Pour dressing over salad and toss to combine.

4. Serve and enjoy!

Nutrition information:
Calories: 190 kcal, Carbohydrates: 21 g, Protein: 5 g, Fat: 10 g, Saturated Fat: 3 g, Cholesterol: 11 mg, Sodium: 170 mg, Potassium: 193 mg, Fiber: 3 g, Sugar: 6 g, Vitamin A: 380 IU, Vitamin C: 11 mg, Calcium: 75 mg, Iron: 1 mg.

31. Buckwheat Stuffed Peppers

Buckwheat Stuffed Peppers are a healthy and flavorful meal, made using wholesome buckwheat, vegetables, and spices. Enjoy this hearty and satisfying dish as a side or main entree.
Serving: 4
Preparation Time: 10 minutes
Ready Time: 30 minutes

Ingredients:
- 2 tablespoons olive oil
- 1 small red onion, chopped
- 1 red bell pepper, diced
- 2 carrots, chopped
- 1 cup cooked buckwheat
- 1 teaspoon smoked paprika
- 1/4 teaspoon garlic powder
- 1/4 teaspoon dried oregano
- 1/2 teaspoon salt
- 1/4 cup vegetable broth
- 4 bell peppers

Instructions:
1. Preheat oven to 350° F.
2. Heat oil in a large skillet over medium heat. Add onion, bell pepper, and carrots, and sauté until tender, about 5 minutes.
3. Add buckwheat, paprika, garlic powder, oregano, salt, and vegetable broth. Cook for an additional 2-3 minutes.
4. Cut off the tops of the bell peppers and remove the seeds. Stuff the peppers with the buckwheat mixture and place on a baking sheet.

5. Bake for 25-30 minutes, or until peppers are tender.

Nutrition information: Per serving: Cal 186, Pro 7g, Total Fat 7g, Carb 27g, Fibre 8g, Sugar 8g, Sodium 391mg, Cholesterol 0mg

32. Buckwheat Veggie Burgers

Whip up a flavorful plant-based meal with these easy and delicious buckwheat veggie burgers. Packed with nutrient-rich Ingredients like black beans, garlic, and onions, they make for a hearty and nutritious meal.
Serving: 4
Preparation Time: 25 minutes
Ready Time: 55 minutes

Ingredients:
-1 cup dry buckwheat groats
-1 can black beans, drained and rinsed
-1/2 onion, finely chopped
-3 cloves garlic, minced
-1/2 teaspoon chili powder
-1/2 teaspoon smoked paprika
-1/2 teaspoon sea salt
-1 tablespoon olive oil

Instructions:
1. Cook buckwheat as per package instructions. Set aside.
2. In a bowl, mash black beans with a fork.
3. Add onion, garlic, chili powder, smoked paprika, and salt and mix until well combined.
4. Add buckwheat and olive oil and mix again until evenly incorporated.
5. Form four burger patties with your hands and place onto a greased baking sheet.
6. Bake at 350°F (176°C) for 25-30 minutes or until golden brown.

Nutrition information (per serving):
Calories: 266; Total Fat: 5.6g; Carbs: 48.2g; Protein: 9.2g; Fiber: 9.2g; Sodium: 523mg

33. Buckwheat Falafel

Buckwheat Falafel is an excellent vegan and gluten-free alternative to traditional falafel. Made with rare and nutritious buckwheat flour, these patties are packed with flavor and perfect as an appetizer or served in pitas or sandwiches.
Serving: Approximately 8 Falafels
Preparation time: 10 minutes
Ready time: 40 minutes

Ingredients:
1 cup buckwheat flour
1 teaspoon baking powder
3 tablespoons nutritional yeast
1 teaspoon ground coriander
1 teaspoon ground cumin
1/2 teaspoon onion powder
1 teaspoon garlic powder
1/4 teaspoon ground black pepper
3/4 teaspoon sea salt
1 cup water
1/3 cup roasted garlic
3 tablespoons olive oil

Instructions:
1. Preheat oven to 375F.
2. In a bowl, combine buckwheat flour, baking powder, nutritional yeast, coriander, cumin, onion powder, garlic powder, pepper, and sea salt until well mixed.
3. Add water and mix into a thick batter. Stir in roasted garlic and olive oil.
4. Use a spoon to scoop out batter and form into 8 balls. Place the balls on a parchment paper-lined baking sheet and lightly press down on them to form patties.
5. Bake for approximately 30 minutes, or until lightly golden brown.

Nutrition information: Per serving (8 falafels): 125 calories, 6 g fat, 16 g carbohydrates, 5 g protein, 3 g dietary fiber, 350 mg sodium.

34. Buckwheat Pilaf

This Buckwheat Pilaf recipe is a tasty and creative way to enjoy a flavorful and nutritious side dish.
Serving: 4
Preparation time: 10 minutes
Ready time: 25 minutes

Ingredients:
1 tbsp olive oil
1 cup finely chopped onions
1 cup buckwheat (roasted or whole)
1 cup vegetable or chicken broth
1/4 cup dried cranberries
1/4 cup sliced or slivered almonds
1/2 tsp turmeric
1/4 tsp ground black pepper
Salt, to taste

Instructions:
1. Heat the olive oil in a large skillet over medium-high heat. Add the onions and cook until softened, about 5 minutes.
2. Add the buckwheat to the skillet and cook until lightly toasted, about 3 minutes.
3. Add the broth, cranberries, almonds, turmeric, black pepper, and salt. Stir to combine.
4. Reduce the heat to low, cover, and simmer for 15 minutes.
5. Remove from the heat and let sit, covered, for 10 minutes.
6. Fluff with a fork and serve warm.

Nutrition information: Per serving: 189 calories, 9.5g fat, 23.6g carbohydrates, 5.4g protein, 3.3g fiber, 6.6mg sodium.

35. Buckwheat Risotto

Buckwheat risotto is a vegan-friendly and delicious twist on the classic Italian risotto. It's made with buckwheat groats instead of arborio rice and is cooked with the same method. This version is flavored with shallots, spinach, and vegan parmesan.
Serving: 4
Preparation Time: 10 minutes
Ready Time: 30 minutes

Ingredients:
- 1 tbsp olive oil
- 2 shallots, chopped
- 3 cloves garlic, minced
- 2 cups buckwheat groats
- 1 tsp Italian seasoning
- 4 cups vegetable broth
- 2 cups spinach
- 1/4 cup vegan parmesan

Instructions:
1. Heat the olive oil in a large pot over medium heat. Add the shallots and garlic and sauté until softened, about 3 minutes.
2. Add the buckwheat groats and Italian seasoning. Sauté for another 3 minutes.
3. Add the vegetable broth and bring to a boil. Reduce to a simmer and cook for 15 minutes.
4. Add the spinach and vegan parmesan and continue to cook for 5 more minutes.
5. Serve the buckwheat risotto immediately.

Nutrition information:
Per serving: 203 calories, 10.2g fat, 24g carbohydrates, 6.6g protein

36. Buckwheat Tabbouleh

Buckwheat Tabbouleh is a healthy, grain-based salad that combines the nutty flavour of buckwheat with crunchy vegetables.

Serving: 8
Preparation time: 15 mins
Ready time: 15 mins

Ingredients:
- 2 cups cooked buckwheat
- 1 large tomato, diced
- 1/2 red onion, diced
- 1/2 bell pepper, diced
- 2 stalks celery, diced
- 2 tablespoons fresh lemon juice
- 2 tablespoons olive oil
- 1/4 cup freshly chopped parsley
- Salt and pepper to taste

Instructions:
1. In a large bowl, combine the cooked buckwheat and diced vegetables.
2. In a small bowl, whisk together the lemon juice, olive oil, and parsley.
3. Pour the lemon mixture over the top of the tabbouleh and toss to coat.
4. Season with salt and pepper to taste.
5. Serve chilled or at room temperature.

Nutrition information:
Calories: 140, Fat: 6g, Cholesterol: 0mg, Sodium: 87mg, Carbohydrates: 18g, Fiber: 4g, Protein: 4g

37. Buckwheat Stuffed Mushrooms

Buckwheat Stuffed Mushrooms are a savory and delicious appetizer that can be served as a side dish or an entree. They are stuffed with a hearty and delicious buckwheat mixture, making this a nutrient-rich and flavorful meal.
Serving: 4-6
Preparation time: 30 minutes
Ready time: 45 minutes

Ingredients:

-1 cup buckwheat groats
-3 tablespoons olive oil
-1 onion, finely chopped
-3 cloves garlic, minced
-1 tablespoon fresh thyme leaves
-2 tablespoons freshly chopped parsley
-1/2 teaspoon dried oregano
-Salt and pepper, to taste
-2 tablespoons lemon juice
-24 large mushrooms, stems removed
-1/2 cup white wine

Instructions:
1. Preheat the oven to 400 degrees F.
2. In a small saucepan, bring 1 1/2 cups of water to a boil. Add the buckwheat groats and reduce the heat to low. Simmer for about 15 minutes, or until all of the water is absorbed.
3. Meanwhile, heat the olive oil in a large skillet over medium heat. Add the onion and garlic, and cook until softened, about 4 minutes.
4. Add the buckwheat, thyme, parsley, oregano, salt and pepper to the skillet. Cook for 3 minutes, stirring constantly.
5. Add the lemon juice and white wine to the skillet. Cook for another 3 minutes.
6. Grease a large baking dish and place the mushrooms in it. Stuff each mushroom with the buckwheat mixture.
7. Bake for 20 minutes.

Nutrition information:
Serving size: 1 stuffed mushroom
Calories: 97 calories
Fat: 5.5g
Carbohydrates: 8.5g
Protein: 2g
Sugar: 0.6g
Fiber: 1.4g
Sodium: 85mg (salt-adjusted)

38. Buckwheat Stuffed Tomatoes

Buckwheat Stuffed Tomatoes is a delicious and healthy vegan side dish that is sure to impress your guests. It is also very easy to make and great for special occasions.
Serving: 4
Preparation Time: 15 minutes
Ready Time: 1 hour 15 minutes

Ingredients:
- 2 tablespoons olive oil
- 1/4 cup chopped onion
- 1/2 cup cooked buckwheat
- 2 tablespoons fresh parsley
- 1/2 teaspoon oregano
- 4 large tomatoes
- 1 cup vegetable broth
- Salt and pepper, to taste

Instructions:
1. Preheat the oven to 375°F.
2. Heat the olive oil in a large skillet over medium heat.
3. Add the onion and cook until softened, about 5 minutes.
4. Add the buckwheat, parsley, oregano, and salt and pepper.
5. Cook, stirring, until heated through, about 2 minutes.
6. Cut off the tops of the tomatoes and hollow out the insides, reserving the flesh for later use.
7. Add the tomato flesh, vegetable broth, and cooked buckwheat to the skillet and stir to combine.
8. Stuff the tomatoes with the buckwheat mixture and place them in an oven-safe baking dish.
9. Bake for 30-35 minutes, or until the tomatoes are softened.

Nutrition information:
Calories: 120
Fat: 5g
Carbohydrates: 14g
Protein: 3g
Fiber: 3g
Sodium: 88mg

39. Buckwheat Veggie Wraps

These hearty Buckwheat Veggie Wraps are the perfect on-the-go meal for when you need something nutritious and delicious of quick!
Serving: 6
Preparation Time: 15 minutes
Ready Time: 25 minutes

Ingredients:
- 12 sprouted multi-grain wraps (or any wrap of your choice)
- 1/2 cup buckwheat groats, cooked
- 2 cups cooked red lentils
- 2 cups cooked quinoa
- 1 bag fresh spinach
- 1 bell pepper, diced
- 1/2 cup vegan feta
- Salt and pepper to taste

Instructions:
1. Preheat oven to 350°F and line a baking sheet with parchment paper.
2. Lay out each wrap on baking sheet.
3. In a medium bowl, combine cooked buckwheat groats, lentils, quinoa, bell pepper, spinach, vegan feta, salt and pepper and stir until all Ingredients are evenly distributed.
4. Place 1/6th of the mixture onto each wrap.
5. Start rolling wrap from one side to the other to form a pinwheel.
6. Bake in oven for 15 minutes or until wraps are lightly brown and crispy.
7. Serve and enjoy!

Nutrition information:
- Calories per serving: 188
- Protein: 9 grams
- Fat: 6 grams
- Carbohydrates: 24 grams
- Fiber: 8 grams

40. Buckwheat Sushi Rolls

Get your chopsticks ready for some delicious Buckwheat Sushi Rolls! Easily prepared in 20 minutes or less, these flavorful and nutritious rolls are sure to become a regular in your weekly meal rotation.

Serving: Makes 6 sushi rolls
Preparation Time: 10 minutes
Ready time: 10 minutes

Ingredients:
- 2 cups cooked buckwheat groats
- 2/3 cup white sushi rice
- 3 to 4 tablespoons rice vinegar
- 2 to 3 tablespoons brown sugar
- 2 nori seaweed wraps
- 2 tablespoons cooked shrimp
- 1 tablespoon cooked smoked salmon
- 2 teaspoons nori seaweed powder
- 1 teaspoon sesame oil
- 1/2 avocado, pitted and sliced

Instructions:
1. Cook the buckwheat groats and sushi rice according to package instructions.
2. In a separate bowl, mix together the rice vinegar, brown sugar, and nori seaweed powder.
3. Once the buckwheat groats and sushi rice are cooked, add them to the bowl and mix until evenly coated.
4. Place a nori seaweed wrap on a sushi mat and spread the buckwheat-sushi rice mixture over the wrap, leaving a 1-inch margin on the top and bottom.
5. Place the shrimp and smoked salmon in the center of the wrap and top with the avocado slices.
6. Carefully roll the nori wrap using the sushi mat to get a tight roll.
7. Cut into 6 equal pieces using a sharp knife.

Nutrition information: Each sushi roll contains approximately 203 calories, 5.5g fat, and 12g protein.

41. Buckwheat Veggie Stir-Fry

Buckwheat Veggie Stir-Fry is an easy and healthy vegan dish made with buckwheat, eggplant, bell pepper and a few spices.
Serving: 4
Preparation time: 10 minutes
Ready time: 20-25 minutes

Ingredients:
- 1 cup buckwheat
- 2 tablespoons oil
- 1 eggplant, cubed
- 1 bell pepper, cubed
- 1 onion, chopped
- 2 cloves garlic, minced
- 2 tablespoons soy sauce
- 1 teaspoon chili powder
- 1/4 teaspoon ground cumin
- Salt, to taste
- Chopped cilantro, for garnish

Instructions:
1. Place the buckwheat in a pot with 2 cups of water and bring to a boil. Reduce heat and simmer for 10 minutes or until the buckwheat is tender. Drain any excess water and set aside.
2. Heat the oil in a large skillet over medium-high heat. Add the eggplant, bell pepper, onion and garlic and cook, stirring occasionally, for 5-7 minutes, until the vegetables are slightly softened.
3. Add the cooked buckwheat and stir to combine. Add the soy sauce, chili powder and cumin and season with salt to taste. Stir to combine and cook for 2-3 minutes, until everything is heated through.
4. Serve garnished with chopped cilantro.

Nutrition information (per serving): Calories: 172, Fat: 7g, Saturated fat: 1g, Cholesterol: 0mg, Sodium: 545mg, Carbohydrates: 22g, Fiber: 4g, Sugar: 4g, Protein: 5g

42. Buckwheat Fried Rice

Feel free to get creative with this easy buckwheat fried rice recipe! Crispy and savory, it's a great way to use up rice that's been sitting around.
Serving: 4
Preparation time: 10 minutes
Ready time: 30 minutes

Ingredients:
- 2 cups cooked buckwheat
- 2 tablespoons oil
- 1 small onion, diced
- 1 red bell pepper, diced
- 2 cloves of garlic, minced
- 2 tablespoons low-sodium soy sauce
- Salt and pepper to taste
- 2 tablespoons sesame oil

Instructions:
1. Heat oil in a large skillet over medium-high heat.
2. Add onion, garlic, and red bell pepper and cook until softened, about 5 minutes.
3. Add cooked buckwheat and stir to combine.
4. Add soy sauce and season with salt and pepper.
5. Cook, stirring occasionally, until everything is heated through.
6. Stir in sesame oil before serving.

Nutrition information: per serving:Calories: 180; Total fat: 12g; Saturated fat: 2g; Protein: 4g; Carbohydrates: 15g; Fiber: 3g; Sugar: 2g; Sodium: 447mg

43. Buckwheat Spring Rolls

Buckwheat Spring Rolls are a quick and easy way to enjoy a delicious vegetable snack. They are made with fresh veggies, buckwheat and other nutritious Ingredients, all wrapped up in a spring roll wrapper.
Serving: 12 Spring Rolls

Preparation Time: 25 minutes
Ready Time: 1 hour 15 minutes

Ingredients:
- 210 g buckwheat
- 345 g mixed vegetables (corn, cabbage, manathakkali, beans and carrots)
- A pinch of salt
- 7-8 spring roll wrappers

Instructions:
1. Begin by cooking the buckwheat. To do this, bring a large saucepan of water to a rolling boil and add in the buckwheat. Boil for 8-10 minutes until the buckwheat is cooked.
2. In the same large saucepan, add in the mixed vegetables. Add in a pinch of salt and sauté the vegetables for around 10 minutes on medium heat, stirring often.
3. Once the buckwheat and vegetables are cooked, place them in a large bowl and mix until combined.
4. Begin making the spring rolls by placing one wrapper on a flat surface. Add a spoonful of the buckwheat and vegetable mixture and top with a few pieces of the vegetables.
5. Wet your finger and run it around the edges of the wrapper, then fold the roll over. Secure the edges and continue this until all the rolls have been made.
6. Heat a large shallow pan with some oil and add in the spring rolls. Fry for 3-4 minutes, turning occasionally, until all sides are golden brown.

Nutrition information: Per Serving: Calories: 140, Carbohydrates: 37 g, Protein: 10 g, Fat: 0.5 g, Sodium: 155mg, Fiber: 7.3 g.

44. Buckwheat Pancake Tacos

Buckwheat Pancake Tacos is the perfect breakfast combination of two traditional favorites — pancakes and tacos. This easy-to-make dish swaps out flour tortillas for buckwheat pancakes, giving it a delicious, nutty flavor.
Serving: 4

Preparation time: 10 minutes
Ready time: 10 minutes

Ingredients:
- 1 cup of buckwheat flour
- 1 cup of milk
- 2 eggs
- 2 tablespoons of honey
- 2 tablespoons of melted butter
- 1 teaspoon of baking powder
- Pinch of salt

Instructions:
1. In a medium bowl, whisk together the buckwheat flour, milk, eggs, honey, melted butter, baking powder, and salt.
2. Heat a griddle to medium heat and grease lightly with a bit of butter or oil.
3. Ladle scant ¼ cup of batter onto the griddle and spread out to 2-3 inches in diameter.
4. Cook for 2-3 minutes until bubbles have formed and then flip to the other side and cook for another minute or two until golden.
5. Repeat with the remaining batter.
6. Serve the pancakes with whatever taco fixings you'd like.

Nutrition information:
Calories: 244 kcal, Carbohydrates: 25 g, Protein: 8 g, Fat: 11 g, Saturated Fat: 5 g, Cholesterol: 95 mg, Sodium: 190 mg, Potassium: 144 mg, Fiber: 2 g, Sugar: 9 g, Vitamin A: 304 IU, Calcium: 128 mg, Iron: 1 mg

45. Buckwheat Breakfast Burritos

Start your morning off with a nutritious and delicious Buckwheat Breakfast Burrito! This vegan-friendly breakfast burrito is full of wholesome Ingredients like buckwheat, tempeh, and vegetables.
Serving: 2
Preparation time: 10 minutes
Ready time: 25 minutes

Ingredients:
- 1/2 cup of buckwheat
- 1 teaspoon of vegan butter
- 1/2 cup of diced tempeh
- 1 cup of diced vegetables of your choice
- 2 tablespoons of olive oil
- 2 tablespoons of tamari
- Salt and pepper to taste
- 2 large tortilla wraps or collard greens

Instructions:
1. Boil the buckwheat according to the package instructions and set aside.
2. Heat the vegan butter in a skillet over medium heat.
3. Add the tempeh and vegetables to the skillet and cook until the vegetables are lightly browned and the tempeh is cooked through, about 10 minutes.
4. Add the cooked buckwheat to the skillet and season with olive oil, tamari, salt, and pepper. Stir to combine.
5. Place the mixture into the center of a wrap or collard green.
6. Fold up the bottom edge of the wrap or leaf and then fold the sides inwards to make a wrap- or burrito-style pocket.
7. Enjoy your Buckwheat Breakfast Burrito!

Nutrition information: Per serving: Approx. 284 kcal, 14 g fat, 5.7 g saturated fat, 11.3 g protein, 33.6 g carbohydrates, 4.7 g dietary fiber, 0.11 g sugar.

46. Buckwheat Quesadillas

Buckwheat Quesadillas are a great way to enjoy a delicious and hearty meal with minimal effort. This fantastic meal is perfect for lunch or dinner, and is sure to please even the pickiest eaters.
Serving: Serves 4
Preparation time: 15 minutes
Ready time: 20 minutes

Ingredients:

- 2 cups cooked and cooled buckwheat
- 1 cup cooked sweet potato, mashed
- 1/4 teaspoon salt
- 1/4 teaspoon black pepper
- 1/4 teaspoon garlic powder
- 2 tablespoons olive oil
- 1 cup grated cheese
- 8 flour tortillas

Instructions:
1. In a medium bowl, combine buckwheat, sweet potato, salt, pepper, garlic powder, and olive oil.
2. Divide the mixture into four equal portions and spread each onto a flour tortilla.
3. Top each with ¼ cup of cheese and fold each quesadilla in half.
4. Preheat a large skillet over medium-high heat and add a tablespoon of olive oil.
5. Place two quesadillas into the skillet, and cook for 3-4 minutes per side.
6. Repeat with the remaining two quesadillas.
7. Cut each into three wedges and serve warm.

Nutrition information:
Per serving - 166 calories, 8.4g fat, 3.2g saturated fat, 14.7g carbohydrate, 10mg cholesterol, 3.3g fiber, 2.9g protein, 548mg sodium.

47. Buckwheat Enchiladas

This delicious Buckwheat Enchiladas dish is an easy and healthy way to whip up a tasty Mexican dinner.
Serving: 6-8
Preparation time: 15 minutes
Ready time: 45 minutes

Ingredients:
- 6-8 corn tortillas
- 2 cups buckwheat groats
- 1 teaspoon chili powder

- 1 teaspoon onion powder
- 1 teaspoon garlic powder
- 1/4 teaspoon paprika
- 1/2 teaspoon sea salt
- 2 cups canned black beans, drained
- 1/2 cup salsa
- 1 avocado, diced
- 1/4 cup cilantro, minced
- 2 cups favorite enchilada sauce or salsa

Instructions:
1. Preheat the oven to 375°F (190°C).
2. Toast the buckwheat groats in a dry skillet for a few minutes over medium heat, stirring occasionally, until they are slightly golden.
3. In a medium bowl, combine the toasted buckwheat groats with the chili powder, onion powder, garlic powder, paprika, and salt.
4. Place a tortilla on a plate and fill with 2 tablespoons of the buckwheat mixture, 1 tablespoon of salsa, 1 tablespoon of black beans, 1 tablespoon of avocado, and a sprinkle of cilantro.
5. Roll up the tortilla and place in a lightly greased baking dish.
6. Repeat with the remaining Ingredients until all the tortillas have been filled and rolled into enchiladas.
7. Pour the enchilada sauce or salsa over the top of the enchiladas and bake in the preheated oven for 25-35 minutes, or until the enchiladas have begun to crisp and brown.

Nutrition information:
Calories: 424.2
Fat: 7.3 g
Carbohydrates: 71.8 g
Protein: 14.3 g
Fiber: 15.3 g
Sugar: 6.3 g

48. Buckwheat Empanadas

Buckwheat Empanadas are savoury pastries that are popular in South American countries. These empanadas are a delicious snack made with a buckwheat pastry and a filling of your choice.
Serving: 6 servings
Preparation Time: 2 hours
Ready Time: 1.5 hours

Ingredients:
- 2 cups buckwheat flour
- 2 tablespoons olive oil
- 1 teaspoon salt
- 1 cup warm water
- Filling of your choice

Instructions:
1. In a large bowl, mix together the buckwheat flour, olive oil, and salt.
2. Gradually add in the warm water, mixing until a dough forms. Knead the dough for a few minutes, then cover and let it rest for 30 minutes.
3. On a floured surface, roll the dough into 12 thin circles. Divide the filling evenly between the 12 circles.
4. Fold the pastry circles in half, pressing the edges together to seal. Once all 12 empanadas are filled, bake in an oven preheated to 400 degrees Fahrenheit for 25 minutes, or until golden brown.

Nutrition information (per serving): Calories: 180, Fat: 8g, Saturated Fat: 1g, Cholesterol: 0mg, Sodium: 270mg, Carbohydrates: 23g, Fiber: 4g, Sugar: 0g, Protein: 5g

49. Buckwheat Pierogies

Buckwheat Pierogies are an Eastern European style stuffed dumpling made with buckwheat flour. These buckwheat filled pastry pockets are so delicious and surprisingly easy to prepare at home!
Serving: Makes approx. 12-15 Pierogies
Preparation Time: 1 hour
Ready Time: 30 minutes

Ingredients:

- 2 cups buckwheat flour/kasha
- 1 teaspoon salt
- 2 tablespoons butter
- 2/3 cup hot water
- 3 tablespoons sour cream
- Filling of your choice (e.g. mashed potatoes, mushrooms, onions, cheese, etc.)

Instructions:
1. In a large bowl, mix together buckwheat flour, salt, butter and hot water.
2. Knead the dough until it is smooth and elastic, then cover and let it rest for 15 minutes.
3. Divide the dough into 12-15 equal portions, then use a rolling pin to roll out each piece into a thin round sheet.
4. Place 1-2 spoonfuls of the filling in the center of each sheet, then fold it in half and press the edges together to seal.
5. Place the pierogies in a pot of boiling salted water and cook for 8-10 minutes, or until they float to the surface.
6. Remove the pierogies with a slotted spoon, then drain them on a plate lined with paper towels.
7. Serve your Pierogies with a garnish of your choice.

Nutrition information:
Serving size – 1pierogi (approx.):
Calories – 75
Total fat – 1g
Cholesterol – 0mg
Sodium – 187mg
Carbohydrate – 14g
Protein – 2.5g

50. Buckwheat Gnocchi

Buckwheat Gnocchi is a classic Italian pasta dish that is a fun and delicious way to enjoy a traditional, hearty comfort food. It's made with buckwheat flour and ricotta cheese, and is the perfect side dish for any dinner.

Serving: 4
Preparation Time: 25 minutes
Ready Time: 45 minutes

Ingredients:
- 2 cups Buckwheat flour
- 1 cup Ricotta Cheese
- 1 Egg
- Salt to taste
- 2 tablespoons Olive Oil

Instructions:
1. In a large bowl, mix together the buckwheat flour, ricotta cheese, egg, and salt until evenly combined.
2. Knead the dough lightly until it comes together, adding more flour as needed.
3. Divide the dough into six equal-sized balls.
4. Roll each of the dough balls out onto a floured surface, shaping them into 12- inch ropes.
5. Cut the ropes into small, bite sized pieces.
6. Heat the olive oil in a large skillet over medium heat.
7. Add the gnocchi and cook for about 5 minutes, stirring often, until they are lightly browned.
8. Serve with your favorite sauce.

Nutrition information:
Serving Size: 8 pieces, Calories: 231, Total Fat: 11g, Cholesterol: 42mg, Sodium: 270mg, Total Carbohydrate: 21g, Protein: 9g.

51. Buckwheat Polenta

Buckwheat Polenta is a classic side dish that's comfort food at its best. Try this simple version with a hint of garlic.
Serving: Serves 8
Preparation time: 10 minutes
Ready time: 60 minutes

Ingredients:

- 2 cups buckwheat groats
- 5 cups water
- ¾ tsp salt
- ½ tsp garlic powder

Instructions:
1. In a medium saucepan add the buckwheat groats and water and bring to a boil.
2. Reduce the heat and simmer for 45 minutes, stirring occasionally.
3. Add the salt and garlic powder and stir well. Continue to simmer for 15 minutes.
4. Serve.

Nutrition information: Per serving: 78 calories, 1g fat, 15g carbohydrates, 3g protein, 1g fiber.

52. Buckwheat Crusted Chicken

Try the most delicious and simple chicken recipe this Buckwheat Crusted Chicken. This oven-baked dish offers a crunchy outer with a succulent center and can be enjoyed with a variety of accompaniments.
Serving: 8
Preparation time: 10 minutes
Ready time: 40 minutes

Ingredients:
- 2 large chicken breasts, pounded into even thickness
- 2 cups buckwheat flour
- 2 large eggs
- 2 tablespoons unsalted butter
- 2 tablespoons olive oil
- ¼ cup milk
- Kosher salt and freshly ground black pepper

Instructions:
1. Preheat oven to 375°F.
2. In a shallow dish, mix together the buckwheat flour, salt, and pepper.
3. In a separate shallow dish, combine the eggs and the milk.

4. Dip each chicken breast into the egg and milk mixture, then coat in the buckwheat flour.
5. Place the chicken breasts on a greased baking sheet and bake for 25-30 minutes, or until the chicken is cooked through.
6. Meanwhile, melt the butter and olive oil in a small saucepan over medium heat.
7. When the chicken is done, remove from oven and brush with the melted butter and olive oil mixture.
8. Enjoy!

Nutrition information: per serving 8, Calories: 275, Fat: 13.2g, Carbs: 14.7g, Protein: 24.6g

53. Buckwheat Fish Fillets

Buckwheat fish fillets are a delicious and savory entrée that show off the flavors of buckwheat, butter, and herbs. It's easy to make and the result is tender, flaky fish and an flavorful buckwheat crust that's sure to please everyone.
Serving: 4
Preparation time: 10 minutes
Ready time: 25 minutes

Ingredients:
- 4 fish fillets, such as bass, perch, or tilapia
- 1/2 cup buckwheat flour
- 1/4 cup melted butter
- 1 teaspoon dried oregano
- 1 teaspoon dried dill
- 1 teaspoon garlic powder
- 1/2 teaspoon salt
- 1/4 teaspoon ground black pepper

Instructions:
1. Preheat the oven to 350°F.
2. Place the fish fillets on a baking dish.
3. In a medium bowl, combine the buckwheat flour, melted butter, oregano, dill, garlic powder, salt, and pepper.

4. Mix until thoroughly combined and the mixture resembles wet sand.
5. Evenly spread the buckwheat mixture on top of the fish fillets.
6. Bake in preheated oven for 20-25 minutes or until fish is cooked through.

Nutrition information: Per serving: 461 calories, 37g fat, 18g carbohydrates, 20g protein.

54. Buckwheat Meatballs

Buckwheat Meatballs are an easy and flavorful dinner or appetizer. The mixture of beef and buckwheat makes for a delicious and juicy flavor that can be served with a variety of sauces.
Servings: 6
Preparation Time: 15 minutes
Ready Time: 30 minutes

Ingredients:
- 1 lb ground beef
- 1 cup buckwheat
- 1/2 onion, finely chopped
- 1/4 cup chopped fresh parsley
- 2 cloves garlic, minced
- 1 teaspoon ground cumin
- 1/2 teaspoon ground coriander
- Salt and pepper to taste

Instructions:
1. Preheat oven to 350 degrees F.
2. In a large bowl, combine ground beef, buckwheat, onion, parsley, garlic, cumin, coriander, salt and pepper; mix until combined.
3. Form the mixture into 1-inch balls.
4. Place the meatballs onto a baking sheet lined with parchment paper.
5. Bake in preheated oven for 20-25 minutes, or until golden-brown.
6. Serve warm with your favorite sauce.

Nutrition information: 193 calories, 10 g Fat, 2 g Carbohydrate, 24 g Protein.

55. Buckwheat Veggie Loaf

This healthy and flavorful Buckwheat Veggie Loaf is an easy vegan main dish that makes a delicious dinner or lunch the next day!
Serving: 6
Preparation time: 30 minutes
Ready time: 1 hour

Ingredients:
- 1 cup cooked buckwheat
- 2 ½ cups cooked lentils
- 2 tablespoons olive oil
- 1 onion, chopped
- 2 cloves garlic, minced
- 1 large carrot, shredded
- 2 celery stalks, chopped
- 2 tablespoons tamari (or soy sauce)
- ½ teaspoon thyme
- ½ teaspoon oregano
- ½ teaspoon basil
- ¼ teaspoon salt
- ¼ teaspoon black pepper
- 1 cup oats
- 2 tablespoons ground flax

Instructions:
1. Preheat oven to 350°F. Lightly grease an 8×4 inch loaf pan with olive oil.
2. Heat olive oil in a large skillet over medium heat. Add onion and garlic and sauté until softened, about 5 minutes.
3. Add carrot and celery and sauté until softened, about 5 minutes.
4. In a large bowl, combine the cooked buckwheat, cooked lentils, tamari, thyme, oregano, basil, salt, and black pepper. Add the sautéed vegetables, oats and ground flax and mix until combined.
5. Transfer the mixture to the prepared loaf pan. Bake for 40-45 minutes, until golden brown and cooked through.
6. Let cool slightly before slicing and serving.

Nutrition information: Per serving: 263 calories, 9g fat, 38g carbohydrates, 10g protein.

56. Buckwheat Lentil Soup

This buckwheat lentil soup is a hearty and healthy vegan dish that is perfect for cold winter days.
Serving: 4-6
Preparation Time: 15 minutes
Ready Time: 40 minutes

Ingredients:
- 2 tablespoons olive oil
- 1 yellow onion, diced
- 2 cloves garlic, minced
- 2 carrots, peeled and diced
- 2 stalks celery, diced
- 1 teaspoon dried oregano
- 1 teaspoon garlic powder
- 1 cup dry green lentils
- 1 cup buckwheat groats
- 6 cups vegetable broth
- Salt and black pepper, to taste

Instructions:
1. Heat olive oil in a large pot over medum-high heat.
2. Add in diced onion, garlic, carrot and celery and sauté for 5 minutes.
3. Add oregano, garlic powder, lentils, buckwheat and vegetable broth and stir to combine.
4. Cover, reduce heat and simmer for 30 minutes or until lentils and buckwheat are cooked through.
5. Season with salt and pepper.
6. Serve and enjoy!

Nutrition information:

Calories: 209 kcal; Carbohydrates: 28 g; Protein: 10 g; Fat: 6 g; Sodium: 564 mg; Potassium: 511 mg; Fiber: 8 g; Sugar: 3 g; Vitamin A: 3185 IU; Vitamin C: 9.8 mg; Calcium: 62 mg; Iron: 3.7 mg.

57. Buckwheat Tomato Soup

Buckwheat Tomato Soup is a healthy and nutritious vegetarian soup! It is full of flavors and is a perfect meal for those looking for a light dinner.
Serving: 4-6
Preparation time: 10 minutes
Ready time: 40 minutes

Ingredients:
- 2 tablespoons olive oil
- 1 onion, diced
- 2 cloves garlic, minced
- 1 teaspoon dried oregano
- 1 teaspoon dried basil
- 2 (14.5 ounce) cans diced tomatoes
- 4 cups vegetable broth
- 1 cup buckwheat groats
- Salt and pepper, to taste

Instructions:
1. In a large saucepan, heat the olive oil over medium heat.
2. Add the onion and garlic and cook, stirring occasionally, until the onion is softened, about 3 minutes.
3. Add the oregano and basil and stir to combine.
4. Add the tomatoes, vegetable broth, and buckwheat and bring to a boil.
5. Reduce the heat and simmer for 30 minutes, stirring occasionally.
6. Season with salt and pepper, to taste.
7. Serve warm.

Nutrition information: Serving size: 1/6 of the soup, Calories: 180, Fat: 6g, Saturated fat: 1g, Unsaturated fat: 4g, Trans fat: 0g, Carbohydrates: 28g, Sugar: 5g, Sodium: 640mg, Fiber: 6g, Protein: 6g, Cholesterol: 0mg

58. Buckwheat Minestrone

This Buckwheat Minestrone is a hearty and healthy soup, perfect for cold winter days. It is packed with flavor from the vegetables and herbs, and the buckwheat adds an extra hearty and unique taste.

Serving: 6
Preparation time: 10 minutes
Ready time: 45 minutes

Ingredients:
* 2 tablespoons extra-virgin olive oil
* 1 onion, diced
* 1 red bell pepper, diced
* 2 cloves garlic, minced
* 4 cups vegetable stock or broth
* 1 (14-ounce) can diced tomatoes
* 1 (14-ounce) can white beans, drained and rinsed
* 1 cup buckwheat groats
* 1 teaspoon dried oregano
* 2 tablespoons fresh parsley, chopped
* Salt and black pepper to taste

Instructions:
1. In a large soup pot, heat oil over medium heat.
2. Add the onion, bell pepper and garlic, and cook for about 5 minutes, stirring occasionally.
3. Add the vegetable stock or broth, tomatoes, white beans, buckwheat, oregano, and parsley.
4. Bring to a boil, reduce the heat to low, and simmer for about 30 minutes, stirring occasionally.
5. Taste and adjust the seasonings as needed.
6. Serve warm and enjoy.

Nutrition information:
Per Serving: 183 calories, 6.7g fat, 25.9g carbohydrates, 8.7g protein, 5.4g fiber.

59. Buckwheat Mushroom Soup

This vibrant buckwheat mushroom soup is the perfect comfort food for cold winter nights. It's hearty, healthy, and naturally vegan.
Serving: Serves 4
Preparation Time: 10 minutes
Ready Time: 40 minutes

Ingredients:
- 1 tablespoon olive oil
- 1 onion, finely chopped
- 500g mushrooms of your choice, chopped
- 2 cloves of garlic, minced
- 1/4 cup white wine
- 1 teaspoon fresh thyme leaves
- 1 teaspoon dried basil
- 1 teaspoon salt
- 2 tablespoons tamari
- 2 tablespoons tomato paste
- 3 cups vegetable stock
- 2/3 cup buckwheat, soaked in water for 2 hours
- 2 tablespoons apple cider vinegar
- 2 tablespoons chopped dill

Instructions:
1. Heat the olive oil in a large pot over medium heat.
2. Add the onion and sauté for 5 minutes, until softened.
3. Add the mushrooms and garlic and sauté for 5 minutes more.
4. Add the white wine, thyme, basil, salt, tamari, tomato paste, and vegetable stock. Bring to a boil, then reduce the heat to low and simmer for 20 minutes.
5. Add the soaked buckwheat and simmer for 10 minutes more.
6. Add the apple cider vinegar and dill and simmer for 1 minute.
7. Taste and adjust the seasonings if necessary.

Nutrition information: Per Serving: Calories 170, Total Fat 5.6 g, Cholesterol 0 mg, Sodium 920 mg, Carbohydrates 25.8 g, Fiber 4.1 g, Sugar 5.2 g, Protein 5.9 g

60. Buckwheat Pumpkin Soup

Experience the comforting warmth of Buckwheat Pumpkin Soup. Be sure to bring a healthy appetite!
Serving: 2 servings
Preparation time: 10 minutes
Ready time: 30 minutes

Ingredients:
- 1 tablespoon olive oil
- 1 small onion, chopped
- 2 cloves garlic, minced
- 2 teaspoons salt
- 2 tablespoons dried thyme
- 1 cup buckwheat
- 1 (15-ounce) can pumpkin
- 4 cups vegetable broth
- 1 cup heavy cream

Instructions:
Goal:
1. In a large pot, heat the olive oil over medium heat.
2. Add the onion, garlic, salt, and thyme. Cook for about 5 minutes, until the onion is softened
3. Add the buckwheat and cook until toasted, about 5 minutes.
4. Stir in the vegetable broth and pumpkin puree.
5. Bring to a boil, reduce to a simmer, and cook for 15-20 minutes, stirring occasionally.
6. Stir in the cream and bring to a gentle simmer for 5 minutes.
7. Taste and adjust seasoning to your liking.

Nutrition information:
Calories: 398, Fat: 22g, Saturated fat: 12g, Cholesterol: 56mg, Sodium: 1547mg, Potassium: 657mg, Carbohydrates: 41g, Fiber: 8g, Sugar: 8g, Protein: 10g, Vitamin A: 197.4%, Vitamin C: 12.1%, Calcium: 10.9%, Iron: 15%.

61. Buckwheat Chili

Buckwheat Chili is a savory and hearty meal that will nourish and delight your taste buds. This vegan and gluten-free chili is packed full of nutrients and protein, and comes together in no time.
Serving: 4-6
Preparation time: 15 minutes
Ready time: 45 minutes

Ingredients:
- 1 onion, chopped
- 2 cloves garlic, minced
- 2 cups vegetable broth
- 1 cup uncooked buckwheat
- 2 cans black beans, drained and rinsed
- 1 can diced tomatoes
- 2 tablespoons chili powder
- 1 tablespoon cumin
- 1 teaspoon paprika
- 1/2 teaspoon cayenne pepper
- Salt and pepper, to taste

Instructions:
1. In a large pot, heat the onion and garlic in 1/4 a cup of broth over medium-high heat.
2. Cook until the onion is softened, about 5 minutes.
3. Add the remaining broth, buckwheat, beans, tomatoes and spices.
4. Bring to a boil and reduce heat to medium-low.
5. Simmer for 30 minutes, stirring occasionally, until the buckwheat is tender.
6. Taste and adjust the seasonings, adding salt and pepper as necessary.
7. Ladle into bowls and serve.

Nutrition information:
Calories: 180, Total Fat: 1g, Sodium: 500mg, Carbohydrates: 34 g, Dietary Fiber: 8 g, Protein: 8 g.

62. Buckwheat Curry

Buckwheat Curry is a delicious Indian dish made with buckwheat, tomatoes, and spices. It is a vegan-friendly dish that is sure to please any food lover.
Serving: 6
Preparation time: 10 minutes
Ready time: 45 minutes

Ingredients:
- 2 cups buckwheat groats
- 2 tablespoons oil
- 1 onion, diced
- 2 cloves garlic, minced
- 2 tomatoes, diced
- 1 teaspoon turmeric
- 1 teaspoon ground cumin
- 1 teaspoon garam masala
- 1 teaspoon chilli powder
- Salt and pepper, to taste
- 2 cups water
- 2 tablespoons chopped fresh cilantro

Instructions:
1. Heat the oil in a large saucepan over medium heat.
2. Add the onion and garlic and sauté until the onion is translucent.
3. Add the tomatoes and spices and cook for about 2 minutes.
4. Add the buckwheat groats and stir to combine.
5. Add the water and bring to a boil.
6. Reduce the heat to low and simmer for about 30 minutes, or until the buckwheat is cooked through and tender.
7. Stir in the cilantro and season with salt and pepper.

Nutrition information: Per serving: 214 calories, 11.6g fat, 25g carbohydrates, 5.6g protein, 4.2g fiber.

63. Buckwheat Coconut Curry

Buckwheat Coconut Curry is a delicious and vibrant vegan dish. It features buckwheat cooked in a creamy and lightly spiced coconut-based sauce. The combination of subtle flavors creates a unique and flavorful curry.

Serving: Serving size: 4
Preparation time: 15 minutes
Ready time: 45 minutes

Ingredients:
- 1/2 cup buckwheat
- 2 cups water
- 1 teaspoon salt
- 1/4 teaspoon turmeric powder
- 1/2 teaspoon ground coriander
- 2 tablespoons oil
- 1 small onion, diced
- 2 cloves garlic, minced
- 1 inch sliced ginger root
- 1 teaspoon cumin powder
- 1/2 teaspoon garam masala
- 2 tablespoons tomato paste
- 2 tablespoons jaggery or brown sugar
- 3/4 cup full-fat coconut milk
- 2 tablespoons chopped coriander leaves

Instructions:
1. Measure and rinse the buckwheat before adding it to a medium saucepan with the water and salt.
2. Bring the pot to a boil over medium-high heat and cook for 15 minutes, covered.
3. While the buckwheat is cooking, heat up the oil in a separate pan.
4. Once hot, add the onions and stir until they start to turn goldenbrown.
5. Add the garlic, ginger and spices, and cook for a few minutes more.
6. Stir in the tomato paste and jaggery, and cook until fragrant.
7. Pour in the coconut milk and bring to a simmer.
8. Once simmering, add in the cooked buckwheat and stir.
9. Turn off the heat and let the flavors combine.
10. Garnish with fresh coriander and serve.

Nutrition information

Calories: 232kcal
Carbohydrates: 24.2g
Protein: 4.2g
Fat: 14.1g

64. Buckwheat Lentil Curry

Buckwheat Lentil Curry is a delicious Indian dish made with hearty mix of lentils, buckwheat, and various spices. It is healthy, gluten-free, and full of flavor.
Serving: 6 people
Preparation Time: 10 minutes
Ready Time: 30 minutes

Ingredients:
- 1 cup dry brown lentils
- 1 cup buckwheat groats
- 2 tablespoons coconut oil
- 2 cups vegetable broth
- 1 onion, diced
- 2 cloves of garlic, minced
- 1 teaspoon ginger, grated
- 2 teaspoons curry powder
- 1 teaspoon ground cumin
- 1 teaspoon garam masala
- 1 teaspoon sea salt
- Pinch of cayenne, optional

Instructions:
1. In a large saucepan, heat the coconut oil over medium heat.
2. Add the onion and garlic and sauté until the onion becomes translucent and fragrant, about 3 minutes.
3. Add the ginger, curry powder, cumin, garam masala, and sea salt. Sauté for an additional 1 minute.
4. Add the lentils and buckwheat. Stir to combine.
5. Pour in the vegetable broth and bring to a boil, then reduce to a low simmer and cover. Cook for 25 minutes.
6. Serve hot with naan or riced cauliflower.

Nutrition information: (per 1/6 of recipe) Calories: 190 kcal, Fat: 5 g, Carbohydrates: 28 g, Protein: 9 g, Fiber: 9 g

65. Buckwheat Vegetable Curry

Buckwheat Vegetable Curry is a flavorful and flavorful vegetarian dish made with buckwheat, vegetables, and spices. This Indian-inspired dish is perfect for a weeknight meal and is sure to be a hit with the family!
Serving: 4 servings
Preparation time: 10 minutes
Ready time: 30 minutes

Ingredients:
- 1 cup uncooked buckwheat
- 2 tablespoons vegetable oil
- 1 onion, chopped
- 2 cloves garlic, minced
- 1 teaspoon fresh ginger, minced
- 1 teaspoon garlic powder
- 1 teaspoon ground cumin
- 1 teaspoon ground coriander
- 1 teaspoon curry powder
- 1 teaspoon ground turmeric
- 1 teaspoon ground cardamom
- 2 cups vegetable broth
- 1 large sweet potato, peeled and diced
- 1 red bell pepper, seeded and diced
- 1 cup frozen green peas
- 1 teaspoon sea salt
- ½ cup coconut milk
- Fresh cilantro, chopped for garnish

Instructions:
1. Heat oil in a large saucepan over medium heat. Add onion and garlic and sauté for 5 minutes, stirring occasionally.
2. Add ginger, garlic powder, cumin, coriander, curry powder, turmeric, and cardamom. Cook, stirring for 1 minute.

3. Pour in the vegetable broth, sweet potato, and red bell pepper. Bring to a boil and then reduce heat and simmer for 15 minutes.
4. Add the peas and salt and simmer for an additional 5 minutes.
5. Stir in the coconut milk and adjust seasonings to taste.
6. Serve with fresh cilantro and a side of cooked buckwheat.

Nutrition information: Each serving of Buckwheat Vegetable Curry provides approximately 265 calories, 13.8 g of fat, 6.9 g of protein, and 26.3 g of carbohydrates.

66. Buckwheat Tofu Stir-Fry

This Buckwheat Tofu Stir-Fry is a delicious vegan dish with gluten-free, nutty buckwheat alongside pan-fried tofu and colourful vegetables for an easy one-pan meal.
Serving: 4
Preparation Time: 10 minutes
Ready Time: 25 minutes

Ingredients:
- 210g buckwheat
- 350 g firm tofu
- 1 red pepper, cut into small cubes
- 1 small red onion, finely diced
- 2 cloves garlic, finely chopped
- 2 tsp oregano
- 1 tsp smoked paprika
- ½ tsp chilli powder
- 2 tbsp olive oil
- 2 tsp soy sauce
- 2 tbsp nutritional yeast
- Salt & pepper to taste

Instructions:
1. Cook the buckwheat according to packet instructions, then set aside.
2. In a large pan, heat the oil over a medium heat and add the onion and garlic. Cook for 2-3 minutes until softened.

3. Add the red pepper, oregano, smoked paprika, chilli powder and tofu and cook for a further 5 minutes, stirring regularly.
4. Add the cooked buckwheat and soy sauce and cook for a further 4 minutes.
5. Finally, mix through the nutritional yeast and season to taste with salt and pepper.

Nutrition information:
Calories: 320
Total Fat: 12g
Saturated Fat: 2g
Total Carbohydrates: 37g
Fiber: 5g
Protein: 13g

67. Buckwheat Quiche

Buckwheat Quiche is a savory French tart made with a buckwheat crust and filled with a creamy mixture of eggs, cream, and herbs. It is flavorful and delicious, and can be served either as an appetizer or main course.
Serving: 8-10
Preparation time: 10 minutes
Ready time: 1 hour 20 minutes

Ingredients:
- 2 cups buckwheat flour
- 1 teaspoon salt
- 5 tablespoons cold butter
- 6 tablespoons cold water
- 1 onion, chopped
- 8 large eggs
- 1/2 cup cream
- 2 tablespoons Parmesan cheese, grated
- 3 tablespoons chopped parsley
- 1 teaspoon thyme
- Salt and pepper to taste

Instructions:

1. Preheat the oven to 350°F. Grease a 9-inch spring form pan or tart pan with butter.
2. In a bowl, mix together the buckwheat flour and salt. Cut the butter into the bowl using two knives or a pastry blender until the mixture resembles coarse crumbs.
3. Slowly add the cold water and stir until it forms a ball. Knead the dough for a few seconds and then flatten it into the greased pan. Bake for 15 minutes.
4. Meanwhile, heat some olive oil in a skillet over medium heat and sauté the onion for 5 minutes.
5. In a large bowl, whisk together the eggs, cream, Parmesan cheese, parsley, thyme, and salt and pepper. Add the onion and mix everything together.
6. Pour the egg mixture over the crust and bake for 1 hour, or until the quiche is golden brown and set.
7. Allow to cool for 10 minutes before serving.

Nutrition information (per serving): Calories: 330, Protein: 11.7 grams, Carbohydrates: 20.5 grams, Total Fat: 21.4 grams, Saturated Fat: 10.9 grams, Fiber: 2.2 grams, Sodium: 258mg

68. Buckwheat Spinach Pie

This recipe for buckwheat spinach pie is a flavorful and nutritious meal that can be enjoyed any day of the week. Made with savory spinach and creamy Greek yogurt, it is a simple yet delicious dish.
Serving: 12
Preparation time: 25 minutes
Ready time: 45 minutes

Ingredients:
- 2 cups buckwheat flour
- 1 teaspoon baking powder
- 1 teaspoon salt
- 1/4 teaspoon freshly ground black pepper
- 3 large eggs
- 1/4 cup extra-virgin olive oil
- 1 cup water

- 1 cup ricotta cheese
- 1 package (10 ounces) frozen chopped spinach, thawed and drained
- 1/4 cup chopped fresh parsley
- 1 cup Greek yogurt

Instructions:
1. Preheat oven to 375°F. Grease a 9-inch springform pan with cooking spray.
2. In a medium bowl, combine the buckwheat flour, baking powder, salt and pepper.
3. In a separate bowl, whisk together the eggs, olive oil and water.
4. Add the egg mixture to the dry Ingredients and stir to combine.
5. Add the ricotta cheese, spinach, parsley and yogurt and stir to combine.
6. Pour the batter into the prepared pan and spread evenly.
7. Bake for 25-30 minutes, or until a toothpick inserted into the center comes out clean.
8. Let cool before slicing and serving.

Nutrition information:
Calories – 180; Total Fat – 10g; Saturated Fat – 4g; Cholesterol – 63mg; Sodium – 500mg; Carbohydrates – 14g; Fiber – 2g; Protein – 9g

69. Buckwheat Stuffed Bell Peppers

Buckwheat Stuffed Bell Peppers are a hearty and satisfying vegan dish that is full of flavor and nutrition.
Serving: This recipe yields six servings.
Preparation Time: 15 minutes
Ready Time: 40 minutes

Ingredients:
- 2 tablespoons extra-virgin olive oil
- 1 yellow onion, diced
- 2 cloves garlic, minced
- 1 teaspoon smoked paprika
- ½ teaspoon dried thyme
- ¾ cup uncooked buckwheat groats

- 2 cups vegetable broth
- 6 bell peppers, cut in half horizontally
- ¾ teaspoon salt
- ¼ teaspoon black pepper

Instructions:
1. Preheat the oven to 375 degrees Fahrenheit.
2. Heat the olive oil in a medium saucepan, then add the diced onion and garlic. Cook for 3 minutes, stirring frequently.
3. Add the smoked paprika, thyme, buckwheat groats, and vegetable broth. Bring to a boil, stirring occasionally. Reduce the heat to low and let simmer for 5-7 minutes until the buckwheat is tender.
4. Grease a 9x13 inch baking tray with oil or cooking spray. Place the bell pepper halves cut side up on the baking tray.
5. scoop the buckwheat mixture in each of the bell pepper halves until it is overflowing.
6. Bake in the preheated oven for 30 minutes.
7. Let cook for 10 minutes before serving.

Nutrition information: Per Serving (1/6): 188 Calories; 7g Fat; 30g Carbohydrates; 4g Protein

70. Buckwheat Ratatouille

A warm and comforting vegan meal, Buckwheat Ratatouille is a simple one pot dish loaded with fresh vegetables and flavorful spices. It's incredibly easy to prepare and packs a punch of flavor and nutrition.
Serving:
6-8
Preparation Time:
15 minutes
Ready time: 35 minutes

Ingredients:
- 1 cup of buckwheat
- 3 cloves of garlic (minced)
- 2 bell peppers (chopped)
- 1 medium onion (chopped)

- 2 medium zucchini (chopped)
- 2 medium eggplants (chopped)
- 2 medium tomatoes (chopped)
- 2 tablespoons of olive oil
- Salt & pepper (to taste)
- 1 teaspoon of herbs de Provence
- 2 tablespoons of cilantro (chopped)

Instructions:
1. Preheat oven to 350°F (175°C).
2. In a large bowl, combine the buckwheat, garlic, bell peppers, onion, zucchini, eggplants, tomatoes, olive oil, salt and pepper, and herbs de Provence.
3. Transfer the mixture to an oven-safe baking dish.
4. Bake for 30 minutes or until vegetables are tender.
5. Sprinkle cilantro over the top and bake for another 5 minutes.
6. Serve warm.

Nutrition information:
calories: 127, fat: 6g, carbohydrates: 13.9g, protein: 3.2g, sodium: 22mg, fiber: 4.2g.

71. Buckwheat Stuffed Eggplant

Buckwheat Stuffed Eggplant is a nutritious, gluten-free vegetarian dish that combines rich and flavorful Ingredients within eggplant boats. This easy and flavorful dish is sure to be a hit with everyone!
Serving: 5
Preparation Time: 20 minutes
Ready Time: 40 minutes

Ingredients:
- 5 medium eggplants
- 2 tablespoons olive oil
- 1 large onion, chopped
- 2 cloves garlic, minced
- 2 cups cooked buckwheat
- 2 tablespoons balsamic vinegar

- 1 teaspoon sea salt
- 1 teaspoon dried oregano
- 1/2 teaspoon black pepper

Instructions:
1. Preheat oven to 375°F (190°C).
2. Slice eggplants lengthwise, about 1/4" thick. Brush them with olive oil on both sides and arrange them flat on a baking sheet. Bake for 15 minutes.
3. Heat 2 tablespoons of olive oil in a large skillet over medium heat, and add the chopped onion and garlic. Cook for about 5 minutes, stirring occasionally, until softened and lightly browned.
4. Add buckwheat, balsamic vinegar, sea salt, oregano and black pepper to the skillet. Stir everything together and cook for 2 to 3 minutes.
5. Divide the buckwheat mixture among the eggplant boats, packing it in.
6. Bake the stuffed eggplants in the oven for 20 minutes more.

Nutrition information:
Calories: 159 kcal, Carbohydrates: 24.4 g, Protein: 5.9 g, Fat: 4.8 g, Saturated Fat: 0.7 g, Sodium: 197 mg, Fiber: 8.6 g, Sugar: 6.5 g

72. Buckwheat Lasagna

This Buckwheat Lasagna is an easy and delicious vegetarian dish that is sure to satisfy everyone. With layers of cheese and vegetables, it is sure to become a family favorite.
Serving: Serves 8
Preparation time: 30 minutes
Ready time: 1 hour

Ingredients:
* 2 tablespoons olive oil
* 1 onion, diced
* 2 cloves garlic, minced
* ¼ teaspoon dried thyme
* 2 cups mushrooms, sliced
* 1½ cups cooked buckwheat
* 2 (14.5-ounce) cans diced tomatoes

* ½ teaspoon sea salt
* 2 cups cottage cheese
* ½ cup freshly grated Parmesan cheese
* 2 large eggs
* 2 cups spinach leaves, packed
* 2 cups grated mozzarella cheese

Instructions:
1. Preheat oven to 375°F. Grease a 9-by-13-inch baking dish.
2. Heat oil in a large skillet over medium heat. Add onion and sauté for a few minutes, until softened. Add garlic, thyme, and mushrooms. Cook until mushrooms are tender, about 8 to 10 minutes.
3. Add cooked buckwheat and diced tomatoes to the skillet. Salt to taste. Cook for a few minutes, until tomatoes are heated through and mixture is thick.
4. In a medium bowl, mix together cottage cheese, Parmesan cheese, and eggs. Stir in spinach and half of the mozzarella cheese.
5. Spread a thin layer of the buckwheat mixture in the prepared baking dish. Layer with half of the cottage cheese mixture and spread the remaining buckwheat mixture over top. Top with remaining cottage cheese mixture and spread the remaining mozzarella cheese over top.
6. Bake for 30 minutes, or until cheese is melted and bubbly. Let cool for 15 minutes before serving.

Nutrition information: Per serving: 445 calories, 24g fat, 36g carbohydrates, 20g protein

73. Buckwheat Ravioli

This Buckwheat Ravioli offers a delicious twist on the classic pasta dish. The buckwheat crepes are filled with a mouthwatering blend of ricotta cheese, herbs, and spices, which create a savory flavor that is sure to please any palate.
Serving: 4
Preparation Time: 10 minutes
Ready Time: 25 minutes

Ingredients:

- 1 cup buckwheat flour
- 1/2 cup ricotta cheese
- 1/4 cup parsley, finely chopped
- 1/4 teaspoon garlic powder
- Salt and pepper, to taste
- 1 egg, lightly beaten
- 2 tablespoons olive oil
- 1/4 cup cold water

Instructions:
1. In a large bowl, mix together the buckwheat flour, ricotta cheese, parsley, garlic powder, salt, and pepper.
2. Add the egg and olive oil, stirring together until all Ingredients are incorporated.
3. Gradually add the cold water, stirring until a thick batter is formed.
4. Heat a skillet over medium heat and lightly grease the bottom with oil.
5. Ladle 1/4 cup of the batter into the skillet and spread it out into a thin circle.
6. Cook for about 1 minute before flipping the crepe. Cook for an additional minute before transferring to a plate.
7. Repeat with remaining batter.
8. Once the crepes are cool, place a spoonful of the ricotta mixture in the center of each crepe and fold in half to form a semi-circle.
9. In a large skillet, heat some olive oil over medium heat.
10. Place the ravioli in the skillet and cook until golden brown, about 2 minutes per side.

Nutrition information:
Calories: 183 kcal, Carbohydrates: 10 g, Protein: 8 g, Fat: 11 g, Saturated Fat: 5 g, Cholesterol: 56 mg, Sodium: 125 mg, Fiber: 1 g, Sugar: 1 g

74. Buckwheat Mac and Cheese

This creamy Buckwheat Mac and Cheese is a delicious vegan twist on the classic dish. Made with buckwheat flour, almond milk and vegan cheese, it is a delicious comfort food that is also healthy.
Serving: 8
Preparation Time: 10 minutes

Ready Time: 40 minutes

Ingredients:
- 2 cups buckwheat flour
- 4 cups unsweetened almond milk
- 3 cups vegan cheese
- 2 tablespoons olive oil
- 2 tablespoons nutritional yeast
- 1 teaspoon garlic powder
- 1 teaspoon salt

Instructions:
1. Preheat oven to 375 degrees F.
2. In a medium bowl, whisk together buckwheat flour, almond milk, olive oil, nutritional yeast, garlic powder and salt.
3. Grease an 8×8 inch baking dish with olive oil.
4. Pour the buckwheat mixture into the dish.
5. Add the vegan cheese and mix.
6. Bake in the oven for 30-35 minutes, or until golden brown and bubbly.
7. Let cool for 10 minutes before serving.

Nutrition information:
Per serving: Calories - 343, Fat - 14g, Protein - 12g, Carbohydrates - 43g, Fiber - 3g, Sugar - 4g, Sodium - 768mg

75. Buckwheat Grits

This hearty and flavorful side dish of buckwheat grits is a great way to add fiber, protein, and nutrition to any meal.
Serving: 4
Preparation Time: 10 Minutes
Ready Time: 25 Minutes

Ingredients:
- 2 cups vegetable broth
- 1 cup buckwheat groats
- 2 cloves garlic (minced)
- 2 tablespoons white wine

- 2 tablespoons olive oil
- 2 tablespoons fresh parsley (minced)
- 1 tablespoon fresh lemon juice
- salt and pepper to taste

Instructions:
1. Bring vegetable broth to a boil in a medium saucepan. Once boiling, add the buckwheat groats and garlic. Reduce the heat and simmer for 12-15 minutes until the buckwheat is cooked through.
2. Add the white wine, olive oil and parsley to the saucepan and mix through. Simmer uncovered for 5-7 minutes until the liquid has been absorbed.
3. Remove the saucepan from the heat and stir in the lemon juice. Season with salt and pepper to taste.
4. Serve warm.

Nutrition information:
Calories: 140; Total Fat: 5.5g; Sodium: 534mg; Total Carbohydrate: 18.8g; Dietary Fiber: 3.2g; Protein: 4g.

76. Buckwheat Stuffed Cabbage Rolls

Buckwheat Stuffed Cabbage Rolls are a savory dish filled with buckwheat groats, veggies, and herbs. This hearty dish is sure to please a crowd!
Serving: 4
Preparation Time: 20 minutes
Ready Time: 1 hour

Ingredients:
- 1 head of green cabbage
- 2 cups buckwheat groats
- 1 small onion, minced
- 2 garlic cloves, minced
- 2 carrots, julienned
- 1 tablespoon of olive oil
- ½ teaspoon of Italian herbs
- Salt and pepper to taste
- 1 cup vegetable broth

Instructions:
1. Preheat oven to 350°F.
2. Start by shredding the cabbage leaves and removing the core. Boil the leaves for about 5 minutes. Once cooked, drain and set aside.
3. Heat olive oil in a pan over medium heat and add the garlic and onions. Cook until softened, about 5 minutes.
4. Add the buckwheat groats, carrots, Italian herbs and enough salt and pepper to taste. Cook for about 5 more minutes.
5. Take a cabbage leaf and spoon a couple of tablespoons of the buckwheat mixture at the stem end of the leaf. Carefully roll up the cabbage leaf and place it in a greased baking dish. Repeat with the remaining cabbage leaves and stuffing.
6. Pour the vegetable broth over the stuffed cabbage rolls.
7. Cover the baking dish with aluminum foil and bake for 20 minutes.
8. Remove the foil and bake for another 20-30 minutes, until the top of the cabbage rolls are golden brown.

Nutrition information: Each serving contains 330 calories, 5g fat, 60g carbohydrates, 9g protein, 6g fiber, and 400mg sodium.

77. Buckwheat Shepherd's Pie

Buckwheat Shepherd's Pie is a delicious and heart-healthy dish that combines buckwheat, vegetables, and plant-based protein to nourish and satisfy.
Serving: 6
Preparation Time:20 minutes
Ready Time:1 hour

Ingredients:
2 tablespoons olive oil
1 large onion, chopped
2 cloves garlic, minced
2 carrots, diced
3 cups cooked buckwheat
2 cups cooked cubed squash
1 cup cooked, plant-based protein

1 cup vegetable stock
3 tablespoons tamari
1 teaspoon dried thyme

Instructions:
1. Preheat oven to 350°F.
2. Heat the oil in a large skillet over medium heat. Add the onion, garlic, and carrot and cook for 5 minutes, or until the onion is softened and lightly browned.
3. Add in the cooked buckwheat, squash, and plant-based protein and stir until well mixed.
4. Add the vegetable stock, tamari, and thyme and stir to combine.
5. Transfer the mixture to a 9x13 inch baking dish.
6. Bake for 40 minutes, or until the top is lightly browned.

Nutrition information: Calories: 220, Total Fat: 4g, Saturated Fat: 1g, Cholesterol: 0mg, Sodium: 390mg, Carbs: 36g, Fiber: 6g, Sugar: 5g, Protein: 10g

78. Buckwheat Chili Mac

Buckwheat Chili Mac is an easy and hearty meal that is sure to satisfy your appetite. This dish is made with buckwheat noodles, kidney beans, tomatoes and chili seasoning to make a flavorful and nutritious dish that is perfect for lunch or dinner.
Serving: Serves 4
Preparation Time: 10 minutes
Ready Time: 25 minutes

Ingredients:
- 2 tablespoons olive oil
- 1 onion, diced
- 2 cloves garlic, minced
- 1 tablespoon chili powder
- 1 teaspoon smoked paprika
- 2 cups vegetable broth
- 2 cups canned kidney beans, drained and rinsed
- 1 cup canned crushed tomatoes

- 2 cups buckwheat noodles
- Salt and freshly ground black pepper, to taste
- 2 tablespoons chopped fresh parsley leaves

Instructions:
1. Heat olive oil in a large saucepan over medium heat. Add onion and garlic, and cook, stirring occasionally, until onion is translucent, about 2-3 minutes.
2. Stir in chili powder, smoked paprika and vegetable broth. Bring to a boil; reduce heat and simmer for 4 minutes.
3. Add kidney beans, tomatoes, buckwheat noodles and season with salt and pepper, to taste.
4. Reduce heat to low and cook until buckwheat noodles are cooked through, about 10-15 minutes.
5. Serve immediately, garnished with parsley, if desired.

Nutrition information: Amount Per Serving: Calories 303, Total Fat 8.7g, Saturated Fat 1.3g, Cholesterol 0mg, Sodium 473mg, Total Carbohydrates 45.7g, Dietary Fiber 11.8g, Protein 12.5g

79. Buckwheat Sloppy Joes

Buckwheat Sloppy Joes are the perfect combination of savoriness and sweetness. Serve up this delicious vegan-friendly dish on your next menu.
Serving: 6-8
Preparation time: 10 minutes
Ready time: 25 minutes

Ingredients:
- 2 tablespoons olive oil
- 1 onion, finely diced
- 4 cloves garlic, minced
- 1 red bell pepper, finely diced
- 2 teaspoons smoked paprika
- Salt and pepper, to taste
- 1 (14-ounce) can diced tomatoes
- 1/4 cup nutritional yeast
- 1 cup buckwheat groats

- 1/2 cup cooked black beans
- 2 tablespoons tomato paste

Instructions:
1. Heat the olive oil in a large skillet over medium heat.
2. Add the onion and garlic and cook for 4-5 minutes, until the vegetables are softened.
3. Add the red bell pepper, smoked paprika, salt, and pepper and cook for 2-3 minutes.
4. Add the diced tomatoes, nutritional yeast, buckwheat groats, and black beans. Cover the skillet and cook for 10 minutes, or until the buckwheat is cooked.
5. Uncover and stir in the tomato paste. Cook for another 5 minutes.
6. Serve hot.

Nutrition information (per serving): Calories: 184; Fat: 5g; Carbohydrate: 25g; Protein: 9g

80. Buckwheat Tacos

These Buckwheat Tacos are a delicious, nutritious, and gluten-free dish. With the perfect combination of Mexican and Mediterranean flavors, this meal is sure to please everyone you share it with!
Serving: 4
Preparation Time: 20 minutes
Ready Time: 40 minutes

Ingredients:
- 1 cup Buckwheat groats
- 2 tablespoons olive oil
- 1 large onion, chopped
- 1 garlic clove, minced
- 2 bell peppers, chopped
- 2 teaspoons ground cumin
- 1 teaspoon smoked paprika
- 1 teaspoon oregano
- 4–5 tomatoes, diced
- 1 cup black beans

- Salt and pepper, to taste
- 8–10 toasted corn tortillas or crunchy taco shells
- Toppings, as desired (like lettuce, avocado, pico de gallo, etc)

Instructions:
1. Begin by cooking the buckwheat groats according to package instructions.
2. In a large skillet over medium heat, heat the olive oil and add the onion, garlic, bell peppers, cumin, paprika, and oregano. Cook until vegetables are softened, about 5 minutes.
3. Add the tomatoes and black beans and season with salt and pepper. Continue cooking until the tomatoes are softened, about 5 minutes more.
4. Take off heat and stir in the cooked buckwheat.
5. To assemble tacos, layer the buckwheat mixture onto toasted corn tortillas or crunchy taco shells. If desired, top with fresh lettuce, avocado, pico de gallo, or other desired toppings.

Nutrition information: Serving Size: 2 Tacos (113g). Calories 263, Total Fat 7.6g, Total Carbs 42.2g, Dietary Fiber 6.7g, Sugars 5.9g, Protein 8.9g

81. Buckwheat Burritos

Buckwheat Burritos are a healthy way to enjoy a wrap filled with plenty of nutritious Ingredients. This recipe uses buckwheat, which is high in protein, fiber, and other essential vitamins and minerals. It also includes black beans, spinach, avocado, and other savory Ingredients for a versatile and flavorful dish.
Serving: Makes 4 burritos
Preparation time: 15 minutes
Ready time: 15 minutes

Ingredients:
- 1 cup cooked buckwheat
- 1 (15-ounce) can black beans, drained and rinsed
- 1 cup thinly sliced spinach
- 1 avocado, diced

- 4 whole wheat or corn tortillas
- 1 tablespoon olive oil
- Salt and pepper to taste

Instructions:
1. Preheat the oven to 350°F.
2. Heat the olive oil in a large skillet over medium heat.
3. Add the buckwheat and cook for 5 minutes, stirring frequently.
4. Add the black beans, spinach, and a pinch of salt and pepper, and cook for 3 more minutes, stirring occasionally.
5. Place the burrito mixture into a bowl and set aside.
6. Place the tortillas on a baking sheet and warm in the oven for 4 minutes.
7. Add the burrito mixture onto the tortillas and top with diced avocado.
8. Roll up the tortillas to form burritos and serve warm.

Nutrition information: per burrito: Calories: 291; Fat: 11g; Saturated fat: 2g; Carbohydrates: 36g; Protein: 10g; Fiber: 9g; Sugar: 1g; Sodium: 370mg

82. Buckwheat Eggplant Parmesan

A delicious, hearty, and easy to make eggplant parmesan using buckwheat for a gluten-free meal option.
Serving: 4 servings
Preparation Time: 10 minutes
Ready Time: 45 minutes

Ingredients:
- 2 eggplants, sliced lengthwise
- 1/2 cup buckwheat flour
- 2 eggs, lightly beaten
- 1/2 cup shredded Parmesan cheese
- 3/4 cup Italian-style bread crumbs
- 2 tablespoons olive oil
- 1 cup tomato sauce
- 1/2 cup mozzarella cheese, shredded

Instructions:
1. Preheat oven to 350°F.
2. Place eggplant slices in a single layer on a baking sheet. Bake for 15 minutes, flipping halfway through.
3. Meanwhile, combine buckwheat flour, eggs, Parmesan cheese, and Italian-style bread crumbs in a shallow bowl.
4. Once eggplant is done baking, lightly brush each slice with olive oil.
5. Dip each eggplant slice in the buckwheat mixture, ensuring it is evenly coated.
6. Place eggplants on a foil-lined baking sheet. Bake for 20 minutes.
7. Top each eggplant slice with tomato sauce and mozzarella cheese. Bake for an additional 10 minutes.

Nutrition information:
Calories: 234, Fat: 12g, Carbs: 21g, Protein: 11g, Fiber: 4g, Sodium: 194mg

83. Buckwheat Stuffed Squash

This delicious recipe is sure to please everyone. Buckwheat Stuffed Squash is packed with nutritious Ingredients, like buckwheat, kale, and squash, to create a savory and healthy dish.
Serving: Serves 4-5
Preparation time: 15 minutes
Ready time: 45 minutes

Ingredients:
- 2 small-medium sized squash, any type, cut in half (and seeded)
- 2 tablespoons olive oil
- 2 cloves garlic, minced
- 1 onion, diced
- 2 cups cooked buckwheat
- 2 cups fresh kale, chopped
- 12 ounces tomato sauce
- ½ teaspoon red pepper flakes
- Salt and pepper, to taste

Instructions:

1. Preheat the oven to 350 degrees F (175 degrees C).
2. Grease an oven-safe dish with olive oil.
3. Place the squash halves cut side up in the oven-safe dish.
4. Heat the olive oil in a large skillet and add the garlic and onion. Cook until softened, about 4 minutes.
5. Add the cooked buckwheat, kale, tomato sauce, red pepper flakes, salt, and pepper to the skillet with the garlic and onion. Stir to combine.
6. Spoon the mixture into the squash halves.
7. Bake for 30 minutes.

Nutrition information: Calories: 172, Total Fat: 7g, Saturated Fat: 1g, Cholesterol: 0mg, Sodium: 77mg, Total Carbohydrate: 24g, Dietary Fiber: 3g, Protein: 5g.

84. Buckwheat Artichoke Dip

Buckwheat Artichoke Dip is a vegan and gluten-free dip that packs a nutritional punch. It is a delightful snack for any party or gathering, as it combines wholesome Ingredients like artichoke hearts, buckwheat groats, and spices.
Serving: 6-8
Preparation time: 10 minutes
Ready time: 20 minutes

Ingredients:
1 cup cooked buckwheat groats
1 can artichoke hearts, rinsed and drained
2 tablespoons garlic, minced
2 tablespoons lemon juice
1 tablespoon olive oil
1 tablespoon fresh parsley, minced
Salt and pepper, to taste

Instructions:
1. Preheat oven to 350 degrees F.
2. In a bowl, combine cooked buckwheat groats, artichoke hearts, garlic, lemon juice, olive oil, parsley, salt and pepper. Mix well.
3. Transfer the mixture to an oven-safe dish and bake for 20 minutes.

4. Serve warm or at room temperature.

Nutrition information:
Calories: 160
Fat: 4 g
Carbohydrates: 21 g
Protein: 6 g
Fiber: 3 g

85. Buckwheat Spinach Dip

This Buckwheat Spinach Dip is a healthy, vegan dip perfect for entertaining or as an addition to any meal. Its combination of buckwheat groats, spinach, and seasonings makes it flavorful and nutritious.
Serving: Serves 4
Preparation time: 10 minutes
Ready time: 10 minutes

Ingredients:
- 1/2 cup buckwheat groats
- 2 cups spinach leaves, coarsely chopped
- 1 teaspoon salt
- 1 teaspoon garlic powder
- 2 tablespoons olive oil
- 2 tablespoons lemon juice

Instructions:
1. In a small skillet, heat the olive oil over medium heat for 1 minute.
2. Add the buckwheat groats to the skillet and cook, stirring, for 2 minutes.
3. Reduce the heat to low and add the spinach leaves, salt, and garlic powder.
4. Cook for 3 minutes, stirring constantly.
5. Turn off the heat and stir in the lemon juice.
6. Serve the dip warm or cold with vegetables and crackers.

Nutrition information:
- Calories: 136 kcal

- Protein: 3 g
- Fat: 7 g
- Carbs: 18 g
- Sodium: 564 mg

86. Buckwheat Hummus

Buckwheat Hummus is a delicious take on traditional hummus, made with a hint of creamy tahini and rich, nutty buckwheat. It is perfect as a dip, in sandwiches, or as part of a mezze platter.
Serving: 4
Preparation time: 10 minutes
Ready time: 25 minutes

Ingredients:
- ½ cup cooked buckwheat
- 2 Tbsp tahini
- Juice of 1 lemon
- 4 cloves garlic, crushed
- 2 Tbsp olive oil
- ¼ tsp paprika
- Salt and pepper to taste

Instructions:
1. Preheat the oven to 350°F (180°C).
2. Spread the cooked buckwheat on a baking sheet and bake for 10 minutes, or until lightly toasted.
3. Put the toasted buckwheat, tahini, lemon juice, garlic, olive oil, and paprika into a food processor and process until smooth.
4. Season with salt and pepper to taste.
5. Serve the hummus chilled or at room temperature.

Nutrition information (per serving):
Calories: 115
Fat: 10g
Carbohydrates: 6g
Protein: 2g
Fiber: 2g

87. Buckwheat Guacamole

Buckwheat guacamole is a delicious and healthy vegetarian snack that is packed with flavor and nutrients. Buckwheat, a gluten-free grain, is paired with avocados and other spices to make a delicious dip that is perfect for chips, vegetables, crackers, and more.

Serving: 4
Preparation time: 10 minutes
Ready time: 10 minutes

Ingredients:
- 1 cup buckwheat
- 2 medium avocados, diced
- 2 cloves garlic, minced
- 1 jalapeno, minced
- 2 tablespoons extra virgin olive oil
- 1 medium tomato, diced
- ¼ cup diced red onion
- 2 tablespoons chopped fresh cilantro
- Juice of ½ lime
- Salt and pepper to taste

Instructions:
1. Cook buckwheat in boiling water for 10 minutes.
2. Drain and let cool.
3. In a large bowl, mash the avocado together with the garlic and jalapeño.
4. Stir in the cooked buckwheat and remaining Ingredients.
5. Add salt and pepper to taste.
6. Serve with your favorite chips or vegetables.

Nutrition information: One serving of buckwheat guacamole contains 140 calories, 9g of fat, 11g of carbohydrates, 4g of protein, 2g of fiber, and 0.7g of sugar. It is a good source of vitamin A, potassium, vitamin C, and magnesium.

88. Buckwheat Salsa

Buckwheat salsa is an easy to make side dish or snack that is sure to impress. Packed with nutritious buckwheat, the fresh flavors of sweet tomatoes, spicy peppers and onion, and a kick of lime juice, this dish is simultaneously savory and vibrant.
Serving: Serves 8
Preparation Time: 15 minutes
Ready Time: 15 minutes

Ingredients:
- 1 cup cooked buckwheat
- 1 medium tomato (diced)
- 1 bell pepper (diced)
- 1/2 onion (diced)
- 2 tablespoons lime juice
- 1 teaspoon cilantro
- Salt and pepper (to taste)

Instructions:
1. Cook buckwheat according to package instructions.
2. In a medium bowl, combine cooked buckwheat, tomato, bell pepper, onion, lime juice, and cilantro.
3. Season to taste with salt and pepper.
4. Serve warm or refrigerate for up to three days and serve cold.

Nutrition information: Per serving: Calories: 63 kcal, Total Fat: 0.3g, Cholesterol: 0mg, Sodium: 9mg, Total Carb: 13.1g, Dietary Fiber: 2.6g, Protein: 2.4g.

89. Buckwheat Cucumber Salad

Buckwheat Cucumber Salad is a delicious and refreshing summer salad. This dish is light and flavorful, making it perfect for lunch or dinner.
Serving: 4 - 6
Preparation time: 10 minutes
Ready time: 30 minutes

Ingredients:
-1 cup buckwheat
-1 cucumber, peeled and diced
-1 red onion, diced
-2 tablespoons olive oil
-2 tablespoons red wine vinegar
-1 clove garlic, minced
-1 teaspoon dried oregano
-Salt and black pepper, to taste

Instructions:
1. Cook the buckwheat according to package instructions.
2. In a large bowl, combine the cooked buckwheat, cucumber, and onion.
3. In a small bowl, whisk together the olive oil, vinegar, garlic, oregano, salt, and black pepper.
4. Pour the dressing over the salad and toss to coat.
5. Refrigerate for at least 30 minutes before serving.

Nutrition information:
Calories: 110
Fat: 5g
Carbohydrates: 11g
Protein: 2g

90. Buckwheat Caprese Salad

Buckwheat Caprese Salad is an Italian-style summer salad, quick and easy to make, and full of flavor.
Serving: 4
Preparation time: 10 minutes
Ready time: 15 minutes

Ingredients:
- 2 tablespoons olive oil
- 2 tablespoons freshly squeezed lemon juice
- 2 cloves garlic, minced
- Salt and ground black pepper to taste

- 4 cups cooked buckwheat, cooled
- 1 ½ cups cherry tomatoes, halved
- 4 ounces mozzarella balls, sliced
- 20 fresh basil leaves

Instructions:
1. In a large bowl, whisk together the olive oil, lemon juice, garlic, salt and pepper.
2. Add the cooked buckwheat, tomatoes, mozzarella balls and basil leaves to the bowl and toss to combine.
3. Serve the salad right away, or chill in the refrigerator for later.

Nutrition information:
- Calories: 262 kcal
- Carbohydrates: 30 g
- Protein: 7 g
- Fat: 14 g
- Saturated Fat: 4 g
- Cholesterol: 15 mg
- Sodium: 120 mg
- Potassium: 228 mg
- Vitamin A: 518 IU
- Vitamin B6: 0.2 mg
- Vitamin C: 8.3 mg
- Calcium: 97 mg
- Iron: 1.7 mg

91. Buckwheat Coleslaw

Buckwheat Coleslaw is a healthy and delicious side salad to enjoy with your meals. It features the healthy benefits of buckwheat, combined with cabbage and beets.
Serving: 6
Preparation Time: 10 minutes
Ready Time: 25 minutes

Ingredients:
- 2 cups cooked buckwheat groats

- 2 cups shredded cabbage
- 2 beets, peeled and grated
- 2 tablespoons freshly squeezed lemon juice
- 3 tablespoons olive oil
- 2 tablespoons honey
- Salt and pepper, to taste

Instructions:
1. In a large bowl, combine the buckwheat groats, cabbage and beets.
2. In a separate bowl, whisk together the lemon juice, olive oil and honey.
3. Pour the dressing over the cabbage mixture and stir to combine.
4. Season with salt and pepper, to taste.
5. Refrigerate for 15 minutes before serving.

Nutrition information: per serving (1 cup): 129 calories, 8.4 g fat, 11.3 g carbohydrate, 3 g protein

92. Buckwheat Potato Salad

This delectable Buckwheat Potato Salad is made with a medley of buckwheat kernels, potatoes, herbs and a tangy dressing that will delight your taste buds.
Serving: 8
Preparation Time: 10 minutes
Ready Time: 1 hour

Ingredients:
- 2 cups buckwheat kernels
- 4 medium potatoes, boiled and cubed
- 2 tablespoons olive oil
- 2 tablespoons red wine vinegar
- 1 teaspoon minced rosemary
- 1 teaspoon minced thyme
- 1 teaspoon granulated garlic
- 1 teaspoon sea salt
- 1 teaspoon ground black pepper

Instructions:
1. In a large bowl, combine the buckwheat kernels and potatoes.
2. In a separate bowl, whisk together the olive oil, red wine vinegar, rosemary, thyme, granulated garlic, sea salt and black pepper.
3. Pour the dressing over the buckwheat and potatoes, stirring until combined.
4. Cover the bowl and refrigerate for 1 hour before serving.

Nutrition information: Per serving: 171 calories, 8g fat, 21g carbohydrate, 2g fiber, 2g protein.

93. Buckwheat Quinoa Salad

This Buckwheat Quinoa Salad combines fresh vegetables and herbs with two protein-packed grains for a light and nutritious side or main dish.
Serving: Serves 4-6.
Preparation time: 15 minutes
Ready time: 15 minutes

Ingredients:
- 1 cup uncooked buckwheat groats
- 1 cup uncooked quinoa
- 2 finely chopped celery stalks
- 1/4 cup diced red onion
- 3 tablespoons finely chopped parsley
- 2 tablespoons chopped fresh dill
- 2 tablespoons freshly squeezed lemon juice
- 1 tablespoon olive oil
- 1 garlic clove, minced
- Salt and pepper, to taste

Instructions:
1. Place the buckwheat and quinoa in separate saucepans and just cover with water.
2. Bring the water to a boil, reduce the heat and simmer, covered, for about 10 minutes, until both grains are tender.
3. Rinse both grains in a colander under cold water.

4. Place the cooked grains in a bowl and add the celery, red onion, parsley, dill, garlic, lemon juice and olive oil. Stir to combine.
5. Taste and season with salt and pepper.
6. Serve warm or chilled.

Nutrition information
Per serving: 156 calories, 5g fat (1g saturated fat), 25g carbohydrate (3g total sugars, 4g dietary fiber), 6g protein.

94. Buckwheat Tabouli Salad

Buckwheat Tabouli Salad is a nutritious, light and delicious salad, full of flavour and texture. It is a great dish to serve as a side, or for lunch or dinner.
Serving: Serves 4
Preparation Time: 15 minutes
Ready Time: 15 minutes

Ingredients:
- 2 cups buckwheat, uncooked
- 2 cups vegetable stock
- 3 large tomatoes, diced
- 2 large red peppers, diced
- 1 large cucumber, diced
- 1/2 cup pitted black olives, roughly chopped
- 1/2 cup mint, finely chopped
- 2 tbsp. olive oil
- Juice of 1 lemon
- Salt and pepper, to taste

Instructions:
1. In a medium pot, bring the vegetable stock to a boil. Add the buckwheat and stir for one minute. Reduce heat to medium-low and cook the buckwheat for 12-15 minutes, until tender.
2. Remove the pot from the heat and drain any excess liquid. Let cool.
3. In a large bowl, combine the cooked buckwheat, tomatoes, red peppers, cucumber, olives, and mint and mix until combined.

4. Drizzle the olive oil and lemon juice over the mixture and season with salt and pepper, to taste.
5. Serve the salad at room temperature.

Nutrition information: per serving - 128 calories, 7g fat, 12g carbohydrates, 4g protein, 4g fiber

95. Buckwheat Broccoli Salad

This Buckwheat Broccoli Salad is a protein-packed side dish made with buckwheat, broccoli, carrots, and crunchy almonds. It's the perfect accompaniment to your outdoor cookout or next potluck.
Serving: 6 people
Preparation time: 10 minutes
Ready time: 35 minutes

Ingredients:
- 2 cups buckwheat, uncooked
- 4 cups broccoli florets
- 2 carrots, shredded or diced
- 1/4 cup slivered almonds
- 2 tablespoons olive oil
- 2 tablespoons apple cider vinegar
- 2 teaspoons Dijon mustard
- 1/2 teaspoon honey
- 1/2 teaspoon sea salt
- Black pepper, to taste

Instructions:
1. Preheat oven to 350° F. Spread the buckwheat on a baking sheet and roast for 15 minutes, stirring occasionally. Once done, set aside to cool for 10-15 minutes.
2. In a large bowl, combine the cooling buckwheat with the broccoli, carrots, and almonds.
3. In a separate bowl, whisk together the olive oil, apple cider vinegar, Dijon mustard, honey, sea salt, and black pepper.
4. Pour the dressing over the salad and gently toss to combine.
5. Serve chilled or at room temperature.

Nutrition information: per serving (1/6 of recipe): 162 calories, 9.4 g fat, 14 g carbohydrates, 6 g protein, 3.7 g fiber, 315 mg sodium

96. Buckwheat Beet Salad

This Buckwheat Beet Salad is a delicious, healthy, and easy-to-make side dish that is perfect for a spring or summer day. Featuring a dynamic combination of flavorful Ingredients and a bright, colorful presentation, this flavorful salad will be a hit at your next gathering.
Serving: Servings: 4
Preparation time: Prep Time: 15 minutes
Ready time: Ready Time: 15 minutes

Ingredients:
- 2 cups cooked buckwheat
- 2 small or 1 large beet, peeled and cubed
- 1/3 cup fresh parsley, chopped
- 2 tablespoons olive oil
- Juice of one lemon
- Salt and pepper to taste

Instructions:
1. Preheat the oven to 375 degrees F.
2. Spread the buckwheat and cubed beets on a baking sheet.
3. Drizzle the olive oil overtop and season with salt and pepper.
4. Roast in preheated oven for 10-15 minutes, until beets are tender.
5. Remove from oven and let cool for a few minutes.
6. Place roasted buckwheat and beets in a bowl and add parsley.
7. Drizzle with lemon juice and toss all Ingredients together.
8. Serve warm or cold.

Nutrition information
- Calories: 144
- Total Fat: 7g
- Saturated Fat: 1g
- Trans Fat: 0g
- Cholesterol: 0mg

- Sodium: 0mg
- Carbohydrates: 19g
- Fiber: 4g
- Sugar: 2g
- Protein: 4g

97. Buckwheat Avocado Salad

Buckwheat Avocado Salad is a light and refreshing lunch or dinner. It is filled with nutritious and fiber-filled buckwheat, creamy avocado and topped with a zesty vinaigrette.
Serving: 4
Preparation Time: 10 minutes
Ready Time: 20 minutes

Ingredients:
-1 cup buckwheat groats
-1/4 teaspoon sea salt
-1 avocado, diced
-2 spring onions, chopped
-1/4 cup pumpkin seeds
-2 tablespoons extra virgin olive oil
-2 tablespoons white balsamic vinegar
-1/2 teaspoon fresh thyme
-Black pepper to taste

Instructions:
1. Place the buckwheat groats in a medium-sized pot and cover with water. Add salt and bring to a boil, stirring occasionally. Reduce the heat to low and simmer for 10 minutes.
2. When the buckwheat is done, drain off any excess water and transfer the cooked buckwheat to a large bowl.
3. Add the avocado, spring onions and pumpkin seeds to the bowl.
4. In a small bowl, whisk together the olive oil, balsamic vinegar, thyme, and black pepper.
5. Pour the dressing over the buckwheat and avocado mixture and gently fold together.
6. Serve the salad warm or chilled.

Nutrition information:
Calories: 257 kcal, Carbohydrates: 19 g, Protein: 6 g, Fat: 18 g, Cholesterol: 0 mg, Sodium: 115 mg, Potassium: 375 mg, Fiber: 5 g, Sugar: 1 g, Vitamin A: 160 IU, Vitamin C: 5 mg, Calcium: 32 mg, Iron: 1 mg

98. Buckwheat Kale Salad

Buckwheat Kale Salad is an easy to prepare and healthy salad made from buckwheat, kale, and a mixture of vegetables. It is light and refreshing and packed with an abundance of healthy vitamins and minerals.
Serving: 4
Preparation time: 10 minutes
Ready time: 10 minutes

Ingredients:
- ½ cup buckwheat groats
- 2 cups kale, chopped
- ½ cup cherry tomatoes, halved
- ¼ cup cucumber, diced
- ½ avocado, diced
- 1 tablespoon extra-virgin olive oil
- 2 tablespoons red wine vinegar
- 1 teaspoon honey
- Salt and pepper, to taste

Instructions:
1. Place buckwheat groats in a medium-sized saucepan and cover with 2 cups of water. Bring to a boil over high heat. Once boiling, reduce heat to low and simmer for 10 minutes or until water is absorbed.
2. Meanwhile, in a large bowl, combine kale, cherry tomatoes, cucumber, and avocado.
3. In a small bowl, whisk together olive oil, red wine vinegar, honey, salt, and pepper.
4. Once buckwheat has finished cooking, add to the large bowl with the other vegetables. Pour dressing over the salad and mix to combine.

Nutrition information: Per serving: 279 kcal, 16 g fat, 23 g carbohydrate, 9 g protein, 7 g fiber.

99. Buckwheat Brussels Sprouts Salad

This delicious Buckwheat Brussels Sprouts Salad is the perfect way to get a healthy dose of nutrients in a tasty and nutritious dish. This salad is made with a variety of healthy Ingredients, such as buckwheat, brussels sprouts, and garlic, and is perfect for lunch or dinner.
Serving: 4
Preparation time: 10 minutes
Ready time: 30 minutes

Ingredients:
- 1/2 cup uncooked buckwheat groats
- 1 lb brussels sprouts, trimmed and finely chopped
- 2 cloves garlic, minced
- 2 tablespoons olive oil
- 2 tablespoons white wine vinegar
- 2 tablespoons Dijon mustard
- Salt and pepper to taste

Instructions:
1. In a large pot, bring 2-3 cups of water to a boil. Add the buckwheat groats and reduce heat to a low simmer. Cook for 10-15 minutes, until the groats are tender. Drain and set aside.
2. In a large bowl, combine the brussels sprouts, garlic, olive oil, vinegar, mustard, salt and pepper. Mix well.
3. Add the cooked buckwheat groats to the bowl and mix until all Ingredients are combined.
4. Serve the salad at room temperature or chilled.

Nutrition information:
Calories: 190, Fat: 9 g, Carbohydrates: 20 g, Protein: 6 g, Fiber: 4 g, Sodium: 135 mg

100. Buckwheat Pear Salad

Enjoy a light and delicious Buckwheat Pear Salad, the perfect accompaniment to your next meal. It has a unique and delightful flavor that is sure to win you over.
Serving: 8
Preparation time: 15 minutes
Ready time: 45 minutes

Ingredients:
- 1 cup buckwheat groats
- 2 pears, chopped
- 2 cups celery, chopped
- 1 cup green onion, chopped
- 1/4 cup olive oil
- 2 tablespoons white wine vinegar
- 1 tablespoon honey
- Salt and pepper, to taste

Instructions:
1. Preheat oven to 375 degrees F.
2. Place buckwheat groats on a baking sheet and bake for 15 minutes.
3. Meanwhile, in a large bowl combine pears, celery, and green onion.
4. In a separate smaller bowl, whisk together olive oil, white wine vinegar, honey, and salt and pepper to taste.
5. Once buckwheat groats have finished baking, add them to the large bowl with the other Ingredients and pour the dressing over top. Mix to combine.
6. Let the salad sit for at least 30 minutes before serving.

Nutrition information:
Serving Size: 1/8 of recipe
Calories: 106
Fat: 7.9 g
Protein: 2.3 g
Carbs: 8.3 g
Fiber: 2.1 g
Sugars: 4.3 g

101. Buckwheat Carrot Cake

This Buckwheat Carrot Cake is a delightfully flavorful and moist dessert that's perfect for any occasion!
Serving: 9 servings
Preparation Time: 10 minutes
Ready Time: 1 hour

Ingredients:
- 1 cup buckwheat flour
- 2 teaspoons baking soda
- 2 teaspoons ground cinnamon
- 1 teaspoon salt
- 3 eggs
- 1/2 cup canola oil
- 1/2 cup maple syrup
- 2 cups finely grated carrots

Instructions:
1. Preheat the oven to 375°F. Grease a 9-inch round baking pan with non-stick cooking spray.
2. In a large bowl, whisk together the buckwheat flour, baking soda, cinnamon, and salt.
3. In a separate bowl, whisk together the eggs, oil, and maple syrup.
4. Stir the wet Ingredients into the dry Ingredients until just combined.
5. Fold in the carrots.
6. Pour the batter into the prepared pan and bake for 40-45 minutes, or until a toothpick inserted into the center comes out clean.
7. Let the cake cool in the pan for 10 minutes before transferring to a wire rack to cool completely.

Nutrition information: Each serving of Buckwheat Carrot Cake contains 209 calories, 10.6g fat, 28.6g carbohydrates, 2.2g fiber, and 4.1g protein.

102. Buckwheat Pecan Pie

This classic Southern-style buckwheat pecan pie is the perfect combination of nutty flavors and crunchy texture.
Serving: 6
Preparation Time: 15 minutes
Ready Time: 70 minutes

Ingredients:
- 2 ½ cups chopped pecans
- ¾ cup dark corn syrup
- ½ cup white sugar
- ¼ cup light brown sugar
- ½ cup buckwheat flour
- 4 tablespoons softened butter
- 3 eggs
- ½ teaspoon salt
- ¼ teaspoon ground black pepper
- 1 teaspoon pure vanilla extract

Instructions:
1. Preheat oven to 350°F.
2. Grease a 9-inch pie plate.
3. In a large bowl, mix together the pecans, corn syrup, sugars, buckwheat flour, butter, eggs, salt and pepper until all of the Ingredients are well blended.
4. Pour the mixture into the prepared pie plate.
5. Bake in preheated oven for 45 minutes, or until the center is set.
6. Allow to cool completely before serving.

Nutrition information:
- Calories: 431
- Carbohydrates: 45g
- Protein: 7g
- Fat: 24g
- Cholesterol: 77mg
- Sodium: 251mg
- Sugar: 34g

103. Buckwheat Apple Crisp

Buckwheat Apple Crisp is an easy-to-make and healthier version of the classic Apple Crisp recipe. This apple crisp recipe is made with healthy buckwheat flour and is a delicious, healthy, and comforting fall dessert.

Serving: 8

Preparation Time: 10 minutes

Ready Time: 40 minutes

Ingredients:
- 3 medium apples
- ¾ cup buckwheat flour
- ½ cup brown sugar
- 1 teaspoon ground cinnamon
- ½ cup cold butter

Instructions:

1. Preheat oven to 375°F. Lightly coat a 9-inch baking dish with cooking spray.
2. Peel and chop 3 medium apples. Place them in the baking dish and set aside.
3. In a medium bowl, whisk together the buckwheat flour, brown sugar, and cinnamon.
4. Cut the cold butter into small cubes and rub into the flour mixture with your fingers until the mixture resembles coarse crumbs.
5. Sprinkle the crumb mixture over the top of the apples in the baking dish.
6. Bake in the preheated oven for 30 to 40 minutes until the top is golden brown.
7. Remove from oven and let cool for 10 minutes. Serve warm.

Nutrition information: Per Serving – Calories: 160, Fat: 8g, Carbs: 11g, Protein: 1g

CONCLUSION

"Buckwheat Bonanza: 103 Flour Recipes"

Buckwheat Bonanza: 103 Flour Recipes has been an invaluable resource for both novice and experienced cooks alike in creating delectable dishes rich in the unique flavors of buckwheat flour. Whether you are looking for breakfasts, snacks, breads, desserts, or savory dishes, this cookbook has an incredible variety of 103 diverse recipes to explore.

The incorporation of buckwheat flour in dishes provides so many health benefits due to the grain's high protein and dietary fiber content, as well as its outstanding nutrient-rich composition, such as essential amino acids like lysine and phenylalanine. The use of buckwheat flour also lends a unique nutty flavor to the dishes that will wow even the pickiest of eaters.

From sweet recipes like Buckwheat Pancakes to savory ones like the Green Olive and Rosemary Pizza, this cookbook provides recipes for not only tasty and flavorful dishes, but also for dishes that are attractive and appealing to the eye. With beautiful photographs to accompany the recipes, you can be sure that you've cooked a masterpiece every time.

We hope that you've had a chance to explore this diverse array of buckwheat flour recipes from Buckwheat Bonanza: 103 Flour Recipes during your gastronomical journey. We encourage you to use buckwheat flour in your dishes for it's nutritional benefits and unique nutty flavor. Bon Appétit!

Printed in Great Britain
by Amazon